'Now, more than ever, we value the importance of our personal health and that of others. If we can learn from this pandemic and apply what we have learnt to better support mental health and wellbeing we will have made progress. The content of this book helps to do exactly that. Containing excellent practical advice from a diverse range of companies, it is a must-read book for anyone who wants to emerge from this crisis with new ideas that enable their business to be stronger and their employees to enjoy more good days at work. A seminal book that will shape the future of work.'
Philip Chin, President Europe, Publicis Health

Managing Workplace Health and Wellbeing During a Crisis

How to support your staff in difficult times

Edited by
Cary Cooper and Ian Hesketh

KoganPage

First published in Great Britain and the United States in 2022 by Kogan Page Limited

2nd Floor, 45 Gee Street	8 W 38th Street, Suite 902	4737/23 Ansari Road
London	New York, NY 10018	Daryaganj
EC1V 3RS	USA	New Delhi 110002
United Kingdom		India

www.koganpage.com

Kogan Page books are printed on paper from sustainable forests.

© Cary Cooper and Ian Hesketh, 2022

The rights of Cary Cooper and Ian Hesketh to be identified as the editors of this work have been asserted by them in accordance with the Copyright, Designs and Patents Act 1988.

ISBNs
Hardback	978 1 3986 0124 6
Paperback	978 1 3986 0122 2
Ebook	978 1 3986 0123 9

British Library Cataloguing-in-Publication Data
A CIP record for this book is available from the British Library.

Library of Congress Cataloging-in-Publication Data
Names: Cooper, Cary L., editor. | Hesketh, Ian, editor.
Title: Managing workplace health and wellbeing during a crisis: how to support your staff in difficult times / edited by Cary Cooper and Ian Hesketh.
Description: London; New York, NY: Kogan Page, 2022. | Includes bibliographical references and index.
Identifiers: LCCN 2021047460 (print) | LCCN 2021047461 (ebook) | ISBN 9781398601222 (paperback) | ISBN 9781398601246 (hardback) | ISBN 9781398601239 (ebook)
Subjects: LCSH: Industrial hygiene. | Crisis management. | Job stress. | Employee motivation. | COVID-19 (Disease)
Classification: LCC HD7261.M226 2022 (print) | LCC HD7261 (ebook) | DDC 658.3/8–dc23
LC record available at https://lccn.loc.gov/2021047460
LC ebook record available at https://lccn.loc.gov/2021047461

Typeset by Integra Software Services, Pondicherry
Print production managed by Jellyfish
Printed and bound by CPI Group (UK) Ltd, Croydon, CR0 4YY

CONTENTS

NOTES ON THE EDITORS

Sir Cary Cooper is the 50th Anniversary Professor of Organizational Psychology and Health at Manchester Business School, University of Manchester. He is a founding President of the British Academy of Management, President of the Chartered Institute of Personnel and Development (CIPD), former President of RELATE, and President of the Institute of Welfare. He was the Founding Editor of the *Journal of Organizational Behavior*, former Editor of the scholarly journal *Stress and Health*, and is the Editor-in-Chief of the *Wiley-Blackwell Encyclopaedia of Management*, now in its third edition. He has been an adviser to the World Health Organization, ILO and EU in the field of occupational health and wellbeing, was Chair of the Global Agenda Council on Chronic Disease of the World Economic Forum (2009–2010) (then served for five years on the Global Agenda Council for mental health of the WEF) and was Chair of the Academy of Social Sciences 2009–2015. Professor Cooper is the author/editor of over 250 books in the field of occupational health psychology, workplace wellbeing, women at work and occupational stress. He was awarded the CBE by the Queen in 2001 for his contributions to occupational health, and in 2014 he was awarded a Knighthood for his contribution to the social sciences.

Dr Ian Hesketh supports Professor Sir Cary Cooper and the National Forum for Health and Wellbeing at Alliance Manchester Business School. He holds a PhD in Management and Social Psychology and an MBA from Lancaster University. His research interests are centred on Wellbeing, Resilience and Transformation and most notably he introduced the concept and phenomenon of Leaveism to explain human behaviours associated with workplace workload and stress. Dr Ian Hesketh is the author of numerous peer-reviewed papers and books in the field of organizational psychology, workplace wellbeing, leadership and resilience.

NOTES ON THE CONTRIBUTORS

James Addison is the UK Head of Operations at JLL. He coordinated and led a multi-disciplinary team in response to the Covid-19 pandemic. James joined JLL in January 2018 and was formerly a Consultant at DXC and PwC.

Charles Alberts is Head of Wellbeing Solutions at Aon in the UK, leading a team of experts who advise employers on people health risk. During his 20-year career he has worked with many diverse organizations to help them achieve their employee wellbeing aspirations. Drawing on his lived experience of mental health issues, Charles is a strong advocate for the role the workplace can play to protect and enhance mental health. He is a Chartered Manager, a qualified Mental Health First Aider, and holds an MSc in Workplace Health and Wellbeing. Charles represents Aon at the Manchester Business School National Forum for Health and Wellbeing at Work and serves on the Board of the mental health charity Dorset Mind.

Prof Dame Carol Black is currently Chair of the British Library, the Centre for Ageing Better, Think Ahead, and NHS England/Improvement's Advisory Board on Employee Health and Wellbeing. Prof Black is also a member of RAND Europe's Council of Advisers, and of the Boards of the Institute for Employment Studies and UK Active. Her professional interests are health, wellbeing, work, welfare, positive ageing and knowledge.

Richard Caddis is Director of Health, Safety & Wellbeing and Chief Medical Officer, BT Group. Richard was appointed Director of Health & Wellbeing & Chief Medical Officer for BT in 2018, to lead the health, safety, wellbeing strategy and delivery for BT group. He is responsible for the development, strategy and implementation and culture change, leading a team delivering the group OHS provision & safety management and assurance programmes for UK and global operations. Richard has worked on global outbreaks (Ebola, Zika, Swine Flu) and is currently leading the pandemic response to Covid-19.

Peter Cheese has been the CEO of the CIPD since 2012, the professional body for HR and people development. He also is Chair of the What Works Centre for Wellbeing and the Engage for Success movement, and has previously chaired the Institute of Leadership and Management and sat on a number of Boards. He writes and speaks widely on the themes of the future of work, and recently published a book, *The New World of Work*.

Anne-Sophie Curet leads Human Resources for EMEA at Jones Lang LaSalle, as well as Corporate Real Estate globally. She also supports the growth of the Sustainability and Net Carbon Zero strategies.

Bruce Daisley is an influential voice on fixing work, published in the *Washington Post*, *Harvard Business Review*, *Wall Street Journal* and the *Guardian*. His book, *The Joy of Work*, was the UK's top-selling business hardback of 2019 and is an international bestseller – now translated into 15 languages. Previously he spent over a decade running Twitter and YouTube (the latter at Google) for Europe, leaving Twitter as its most senior leader outside of the United States. Bruce runs the Apple #1 Business Chart-topping podcast *Eat Sleep Work Repeat* on work culture. His second book, about how we think about resilience incorrectly, is out in 2022.

Nick Davison is Head of Health Services, John Lewis Partnership. Nick joined the John Lewis Partnership in 2011 with a brief to redesign and create a health service to reflect the changing needs of this leading retailer and support the health of its 90,000 co-owning Partners. Nick's passion for service improvement has driven the new service, which launched in 2013. The unique shared service model blends an in-house team, who act as the integrators, with specialist providers and has resulted in better clinical outcomes for individuals, increased business productivity, and a lower cost of delivery. Nick previously held roles as Head of Strategy, Aviva Health, and General Manager, Occupational Health, also at Aviva, and has considerable change management experience from the financial service industry. Nick has an MBA from Henley Business School where he majored in the impact of strategic innovation and disruptive forces.

Jennifer Gardner is the Assistant Director at NHS Employers. Jennifer leads the work of the development and employment team, specifically on staff experience. This includes the wellbeing of the workforce, staff engagement, retention, and promoting cultures of civility and respect. Jennifer is a key representative with networks and stakeholders, driving forward NHS Employers' programmes of work across the UK. Jennifer brings a wealth of experience and expertise in tackling workforce issues to NHS Employers, having worked for the NHS throughout her career where she specialized in human resources, staff wellbeing and reducing sickness absence. This work was recognized nationally and received a number of awards. Jennifer is a coach and chartered fellow of the Chartered Institute of Personnel and Development.

Jenny Gowans is the Director of Research, Policy and Content at the CIPD, the professional body for HR and people development. She uses her 20+ year media background to ensure policy makers, people professionals and organizations can get the evidence and resources they need to enable better work for all – something she is very passionate about.

Dr Sally Hemming is the Employee Relations Director for EMEA at Jones Lang LaSalle and an academic researcher. Her research interests include the self-management support needs of workers with long-term health conditions, including Covid-19 recovery, and the psychosocial work environment.

Suzanne Horne is a partner and vice-chair of Paul Hastings' London office, and co-chair of its diversity committee. As head of the Firm's International Employment practice, she advises global employers on how to successfully navigate the complex and dynamic international law landscape on the full range of HR and employment law issues, including employee privacy issues. She is regularly quoted in the national press about topical employment law matters and has appeared on national television and radio. In June she was named

'Labour and Employment Lawyer of the Year' at the Women in Business Law Awards Europe 2021, which recognizes the leading women lawyers from across Europe.

Sir Chris Husbands is Vice-Chancellor of Sheffield Hallam University, one of the UK's largest and most diverse universities. He has an academic background in global education policy and practice. He has led education improvement initiatives around the world, and as the Chair of the Teaching Excellence and Student Outcomes Framework (TEF) leads the UK Government's flagship initiative on improving teaching in higher education.

Dr Paul Litchfield CBE is an experienced occupational physician who has held multiple roles in the public and private sector (eg former CMO of BT). He is currently independent Chief Medical Adviser to ITV and Compass Group plc as well as a member of the HSE Workplace Health Expert Committee. Paul is also a visiting professor at Coventry University.

Kelly Metcalf Chartered FCIPD is the Head of Diversity, Inclusion and Wellbeing for Fujitsu Northern & Western Europe. Kelly is passionate about creating an environment where everyone can be completely themselves at work and advocates the positive connection between employee wellbeing and inclusion. Recognizing the benefits to wellbeing and increasing diversity that supportive flexible working can bring, Kelly is also leading on Fujitsu's future ways of working beyond the Covid-19 pandemic. During her time at Fujitsu, Kelly has worked in a variety of HR roles including Head of Organization Design and Change, and European-wide HR Generalist roles. She spent her early career as an HR Graduate at BAE Systems and achieved her BSc Hons in Management at UMIST.

Andy Rhodes QPM is the former Chief Constable of Lancashire Police and together with Dr Ian Hesketh founded the National Police Wellbeing Service, Oscar Kilo, in 2015. Oscar Kilo is now a government-funded service supporting over 200,000 police personnel and Andy has recently been appointed as the Service Director.

Dr David Roomes is the Chief Medical Officer for Rolls-Royce plc. David is responsible for leading the Global Health, Safety, Wellbeing and Environment Function at Rolls-Royce. Previous roles were with Rio Tinto (mining), GlaxoSmithKline (pharmaceuticals) and the NHS. As part of the Rolls-Royce People Leadership Team, David is currently focused on embedding workforce wellbeing as an enabler to enhance engagement, productivity and performance. David is a practising physician and is a Fellow of the Royal College of Physicians, the Faculty of Occupational Medicine, and the American College of Occupational and Environmental Medicine. His special interest is workplace mental health and wellbeing.

Karen Sancto manages the employee benefits and wellbeing programme for Microsoft UK. Karen has a passion for driving inclusivity in benefits and delivering a proactive wellbeing programme to support employees at all stages of their lifecycle. She's looking forward to the next phase of the hybrid workplace and the innovations in technology that will support the new ways of working.

Kerrie Smith is an associate director for health and wellbeing at Mace Construction. She was trained in occupational and business psychology at Kingston Business School and prior to Mace was managing a research project for the Money Advice Service on the impact of financial education on low-income workers across London. Prior to that, Kelly worked in corporate wellbeing roles, predominantly across the insurance industry. Kerrie says construction was always on her hit list and now she has the goal that by 2026 she will have her teams leaving work healthier and safer than when they arrived.

Brad Taylor is MD and Founder of Strategically People Ltd. Previously Director of People, OD and Workplace at the CIPD, the professional body for HR and people development, Brad has led HR and leadership development in Europe, Africa and Asia and co-led the cultural integration of the joint venture between CIMA and the AICPA. Brad holds a Postgraduate Diploma in Personnel Management from Kingston University and is a Chartered Fellow of the CIPD.

Tony Vickers-Byrne, Chartered FCIPD, was Public Health England's first HR Director and was the Chief Adviser for HR Practice at the

Chartered Institute of Personnel and Development. Tony is currently the Chief Adviser to the Board of Armstrong Craven, a global talent mapping, pipelining and executive search partner for scarce and senior positions, and a Trustee at the Royal Society for Public Health.

Introduction

During a crisis, there are many aspects of business that suffer, but it is people and their mental health who often bear the brunt. Levels of stress, anxiety, insecurity and instability in employees all increase, which if unmanaged can result in an unsettled and unproductive workforce – the exact opposite of what an organization requires to overcome a crisis. If organizations prioritize the health and wellbeing of their staff then they can not only survive a crisis but come out of it stronger than before. Written and edited by Professor Sir Cary Cooper and Dr Ian Hesketh, this is a practical book for HR professionals, business leaders and anyone responsible for talent management who needs to deal with workplace health and wellbeing.

Detailing a view from a diverse group of organizations, the accounts provided in this book give a fascinating insight into the challenges and coping mechanisms of a variety of industry sectors. This book describes how several organizations operating in the UK responded to an unprecedented crisis: the coronavirus outbreak during 2020 and 2021. This book has an emphasis on the state in the UK, although the situation around the globe was, and is, undoubtedly similar. This global catastrophe altered the trajectory of almost every organization on the planet and set us all on a different path in both our home and our working lives. The impact of the crisis will be felt for decades to come. New ways of living and working have had to be adopted, almost overnight. The scale and pace at which organizations have had to change and adapt was simply unthinkable and literally inconceivable just a few years ago.

The organizations contributing to this book cover a range of business sectors, sizes and make-ups. This provides a unique and truly fascinating picture of how organizations with employees in the UK addressed the crisis. The common factor is that they are all members of the National Forum for Health and Wellbeing at Work, based in the UK. The Forum was conceived in December 2015 by Professor Sir Cary Cooper, 50th Anniversary Professor of Organizational Psychology and Health at Alliance Manchester Business School, and Dr Paul Litchfield, the then Chief Medical Officer for BT. In 2016 the Forum was launched and now (2021) consists of around 40 major large and global organizations.

The Forum is focused on improving workplace wellbeing in the UK and globally. The ambition is to inspire people and organizations to challenge their thinking about the opportunities that healthy and high-performing people bring to work, and create shared values that both business and people can realize. The Forum aims to bring the most innovative evidence-based thinking to organizations, as well as to integrate the psychosocial determinants of health drivers of business performance.

Overview

Within this book we will explain how Forum members managed the wellbeing of their own workforces before, during and after the crisis, including what went well, what didn't, and what they will take forward – the organizational learning from crises. This book will also comment on likely future work scenarios and enquire how organizations will learn to work in a new realm. The criticality of socially skilled managers, work-life integration and the influence of technology will all play a key part in future working life.

This book opens in Chapter 1 with a brief look at working life prior to the pandemic and the focus of the National Forum. We also hear about the financial situation pre-pandemic and, although it was stable, as you will hear, there were not many signs of huge growth areas in any particular business sectors. Andy Haldane, Chief Executive of the Royal Society of Arts and former Chief Economist of the Bank of England, provided the Forum with an insightful reflection on the state of the economy before Covid-19. The chapter concludes with a view of previous pandemic experiences.

Chapter 2 is concerned with the impact of the lockdown in the UK, particularly the huge change in working practices that emerged from this, including some of the new language born out of the pandemic. Terms such as social distancing, quarantining, isolating and shielding are discussed, as well as the new technologies employed for working at home, including Zoom, Teams and Skype, and numerous other platforms that enabled work to continue, albeit in a very different way.

Chapter 3 gets into the valuable content of this book with the first of the sector views. Here Andy Rhodes, the former Chief Constable of Lancashire Constabulary, reflects on his time leading a police force as the pandemic struck. Likening it to the VUCA world described by Casey (speaking in relation to the conflicts in Afghanistan and Iraq), Andy gives an honest account of executive decision making during the pandemic. This hinges on being told what is actually happening, and how people are reacting in both their work and home lives. This provides a fascinating insight and draws upon years of experience in policing emergencies, crises, disasters and many major incidents. Andy concedes that none of these can be compared to the Covid-19 pandemic and the impact it has had on society and the workforce. Andy concludes with some reflections on 'So what?' and 'What happens now?' and how we can take new working practices forward as the pandemic subsides and we move into the recovery stages.

Chapter 4 contains a case study from Kelly Metcalf, the head of diversity, inclusion and wellbeing for Northern and Western Europe for Fujitsu, a Japanese multinational information technology equipment and service company headquartered in Tokyo. Kelly outlines her experiences working for Fujitsu prior to the pandemic and also the impact that the pandemic had on the technology sector more broadly, for example, the soaring demand for home working solutions. In particular, Kelly focuses on the company being able to quickly enable home working for its own people while acknowledging that working from home has far more elements to it than simply using technology to enable working. She cites human factor issues that impact on people's wellbeing at Fujitsu, and like the majority of contributors within this book, she also identifies the key role of line managers within the work paradigm. She proposes that flexibility became the default setting while the pandemic spread and home working was the go-to solution for most organizations. She also points out the critical importance of an inclusive working environment, including an open mental health culture.

Chapter 5 of this book is written by Bruce Daisley, the former European vice president for Twitter and the author of the number one business podcast, *Eat Sleep Work Repeat*. Bruce gives us an insightful view of his experiences when the pandemic struck. He goes on to talk about his thoughts on the concept of fortitude, when viewed in terms of resilience. Bruce provides some insight into what resolute people can do in organizations, particularly in relation to Control, Identity and Community. He posits that connectedness with others makes us far stronger. He concludes that the coronavirus pandemic has given us a timely opportunity to reconsider how we may think about resilience.

Chapter 6 of this book contains an account from Sir Chris Husbands, the vice-chancellor of Sheffield Hallam University. Like other contributors to this book, Chris recalls that almost overnight he had to transition the university to an entirely different way of working altogether. His ability to have on-site oversight of the university was taken from him and the organization, one of the largest universities in the UK, was forced to become a largely remote operation. Like most organizational executives, Chris had to rely on relatively few of his number to come up with creative mobile solutions. His aim was to reassure both staff and students that the university was right behind them, and he also was tested with trying to work out what a home working solution would look like in practice. How would the staff and students find a secure safe place to work from? How would they tackle age-old problems such as weak broadband signals? Chris leaned heavily on his life-long academic experience and turned to leadership to overcome the consequences of the pandemic, ensuring that the experiences of both staff and students were as good as he could feasibly make them. Chris concludes with reflections on what the 'new' post-pandemic university experience may look like.

The seventh chapter of this book is written by Jennifer Gardner from NHS Employers. Jennifer is the assistant director and provides fantastic insight into how an already strained NHS coped with the sheer workloads that the pandemic threw at them. This involved amazing staff doing an amazing job in the face of a very challenging pandemic. Jennifer describes a three-phased approach – the critical, aftermath and recovery phases – and concludes with some examples of what NHS trusts have done to improve staff wellbeing during the period of the pandemic, speculating on what may come next for NHS Employers.

Chapter 8 provides insight from Microsoft. Karen Sancto outlines two company expectations: high impact and a growth mindset. By its very nature, Microsoft is already a remote working solutions expert, but what the pandemic brought was a laser focus on empathic communications, wellbeing and practical pandemic policies. Karen details how they went about this, and she concludes with some reflections on how the pandemic has accelerated transformation in many areas of business.

In Chapter 9, Kerrie Smith outlines the approach of the construction industry, namely Mace Construction. She outlines that Mace use engagement surveys to gain employee voice, and from this create Gold, Silver and Bronze resilience groups to shape their response to Covid-19 and to manage the crisis on a global level. Kerrie goes on to describe facets of Mace's 'Protect our People' plan to address new and emerging health and wellbeing risks posed by the pandemic. Kerrie talks about the many additional provisions put in place over the pandemic, including a three-month-long campaign called 'Getting personal with... positive psychology', with a focus on improving happiness, building on individual strengths and the things that keep people well. The proactive campaign wasn't to 'make light' of the very real risks to mental health and wellbeing at the time; they acknowledged that everyone had been impacted in one way or another, but they also wanted to do more by looking at mental health through a different, more positive, and proactive lens, so that they were better equipped to tackle negative mental health before it became an issue. Kerrie concludes with Mace's plan for the health and wellbeing team, in collaboration with key stakeholders, being in the process of developing a new strategic plan that will redefine their approach to health and wellbeing. The plan will contribute to the successful delivery of both the business strategy to 2026 and the health, safety and wellbeing strategy to 2026, and will be underpinned by intelligent data and informed by Mace colleagues from across the business and supply chain to create more good days at work for all.

The CIPD supports many organizations and in Chapter 10 we hear how this pivoted to accommodate the huge demands of the pandemic. By the end of March 2020, the CIPD had launched a dedicated coronavirus hub on their website. This resource saw more than 2.2 million unique users, over 4 million page views, and 158,000 downloads in the first four months and continued to be a source of support through webinars, factsheets and guides updated daily to millions. CIPD began to tailor their services, realizing that a short time into the pandemic most employees and workers had fallen into one of three camps: essential workers working from their usual places of work on the frontline, those able to work from home operating in a virtual world, and those for whom work was drying up and who were already worrying about their futures. Reassessing business models, financial forecasting and scenario planning became critical and frequent. It was clear that sustaining jobs was going to be a challenge. Rapid innovation was going to be needed. The CIPD called on employers to put the wellbeing and financial security of their people first, and on policymakers to support businesses to do the right thing. They were quick to call for a UK Job Retention Scheme and among the first to suggest it be made as flexible as possible.

Chapter 11 is an account from David Roomes at Rolls-Royce, who need little in the way of introduction but who have taken an enormous hit from the pandemic, specifically within the aviation sector. With an approximately 50 per cent market share of the large aero engine market, Rolls-Royce derives a significant proportion of its revenue from long-haul air travel. As such it is understandable that the workforce experienced enormous uncertainty, insecurity and isolation. For some people, loss and bereavement have been ever-present risks to psychological wellbeing throughout the pandemic. Additional pressures have come in the form of home-schooling for some and concerns over the wellbeing of elderly and vulnerable loved ones for many. The strain on personal relationships has been highlighted by published statistics regarding increases in domestic violence, and a key part of any business response had to be that any vulnerable employee had access to the security of the workplace should they need it. David outlines the resources and support put in place to manage this onslaught, including a 'Covid microsite' which was set up on the intranet homepage with the understanding that this would become the 'single source of truth' and one-stop shop for all resources relating to the pandemic.

Nick Davison from the John Lewis partnership provides a dichotomy in Chapter 12. The partnership has the two well-known household names, John Lewis and Waitrose. The nature of Waitrose as a food retailer and John Lewis as a non-food retailer meant that the business could not operate consistently as one during the pandemic restrictions, with Waitrose trading throughout as an essential retailer and to help 'feed the nation', while John Lewis as a non-essential retailer was forced to close for extended periods before finally reopening in April 2021. Waitrose Partners working on the shop floor experienced the extremes of customer behaviours as people panicked, sometimes over the least obvious items. Unsurprisingly, there was immediate pressure on Waitrose.com for a significant increase in online grocery and delivery orders. Typically, at the start of the pandemic, Waitrose was delivering 60,000 orders per week to customers' homes, but this was soon scaled to 240,000 weekly deliveries. Nick promotes a benefit of being one Partnership with two brands, which is that more than 4,500 Partners from John Lewis could be redeployed to Waitrose during the various lockdowns, helping to keep the nation fed and help as absence levels rose.

Chapter 13 is an account from JLL, a global real estate services company employing over 90,000 workers across 80 countries, and who buy, build, occupy and invest in various assets including industrial, commercial, retail, residential and hotel real estate. Sally Hemming opens up with an overview of where the organization found itself as the pandemic hit. Anne-Sophie Curet, Head of People & Spaces, then continues to describe how operationally they moved to home working and began mapping their wellbeing roadmap, delivering their first wellbeing modules very quickly. JLL knew that managers needed guidance in managing remote teams and that employees needed guidance about remote working. JLL conceded that they had moved into people's private sphere, their homes. However, they found that people discovered emotions and started to speak more and were more humbling, sharing when they were feeling good or awful. People spoke more about their wellbeing and were accepting of others. James Addison, the head of UK operations, concludes the chapter, noting that working parents at JLL, some of whom did not have support bubbles, seemed to suffer most. He acknowledges this was an unbelievably difficult time and many people felt that they were not winning in either role. James explains how they developed strong support networks, mainly on Teams, and advised safeguards to their people to help mitigate long periods online – moving to walking meetings, reducing to 25- or 50-minute meetings to enable breaks, encouraging daily exercise, and offering free Headspace subscriptions. Yet despite these safeguards, JLL have had to be largely home-based, and with nowhere else to go, the boundaries between work and home seemed to have evaporated.

Suzanne Horne is a Partner and Vice-Chair of the London Office of Paul Hastings LLP, one of the leading law firms in the world, with 21 global offices across Europe, Asia, Latin America and the United States and around 1,600 employees. In Chapter 14, Suzanne describes the journey through the pandemic, stating that the transition to remote working was relatively seamless as they had learnt along the way as other countries locked down and began to work remotely. Suzanne tells how numerous communications conveyed information, plans and results, which had the effect of motivating and reassuring; they emphasized the importance of the health and wellbeing of the entire Paul Hastings community, acknowledging the challenges faced by all. They reiterated time and time again the importance for partners, managers and team leaders to connect, reach out and engage with their teams and clients. Like so many organizations, some employees live alone, some share flats where there isn't a dedicated workspace or equipment, and some needed to redefine the divide between home and work for their own wellbeing. Having spent such considerable time focusing on physical health and wellbeing and the risks of contracting Covid-19, Paul Hastings rightly saw a redress of the balance to also acknowledge the mental toll colleagues were experiencing from isolation and remoteness during the crisis. In returning to the office, Suzanne noted there was a wonderful camaraderie and warmth from seeing colleagues again on what felt like the other side of the crisis. Even though a further lockdown returned employees back home, the organization has a commitment to return all the workforce to the office post-pandemic. This is as important for helping to nurture and strengthen their sense of culture, teamwork and collaboration as it is for serving their clients at the highest levels.

In Chapter 15, Charles Alberts, the wellbeing manager for Aon, speculates that the pandemic has accelerated many work-related trends and that some of these trends are likely to become business as usual in the future. He discusses flexible working practices and previous taboos, such as mental health in the workforce, which he suggests are now regularly discussed with managers. Charles stresses the critical role good managers play in the wellbeing of the workforce.

In Chapter 16, Professor Dame Carol Black and her colleagues outline the impact of Covid-19 on the older workforce. They provide details of issues such as that of unemployment in the ageing workforce, juxtaposing the situation prior to the pandemic in areas such as hazards and risks of unemployment. Here we also see some graphic illustrations from national modelling of unemployment by age groups as well as analysis from the Office for National Statistics (ONS). Also contained within this chapter is an overview of the working population and the impact of furloughing and shielding on those in different age groups and different industry sectors. At the conclusion of this chapter there are case studies from BT, Thames Water and Microsoft illustrating the extent to which some of this has changed. The chapter concludes with an overview of the impact that the pandemic has had on future policy and practice.

01

Before the outbreak

National Forum for Health and Wellbeing at Work

The work of the Forum pre-pandemic was focused around seeking out best practice, listening to members' experiences and trying to understand the world of work in ways that may improve meaning and purpose for the workforce – the key tenets of wellbeing. This listening allowed the Forum members to find out what would actually be useful for them in terms of the wellbeing of their organizations and people. Pre-Covid, the big issues were around the large amount of mental ill-health in the workplace, which was the leading cause of sickness absence. Issues around presenteeism and leaveism were also widely cited (see for example CIPD Health and Wellbeing at Work Survey, 2021). Undoubtedly, the pandemic has changed everything. For example, pre-Covid, people were saying they wanted more flexible working; Covid has accelerated this and other aspects of working, such as remote working, at warp speed. Other aspects of the Forum's early focus were very much around technology in the workplace, the working environment, compassion and empathy in the workplace, the experience for young people and the impact of line managers. The Forum had workstreams looking at all these workplace challenges and produced guidance and advice that were shared widely. The Forum also invited key speakers to share their knowledge and experience from their areas of expertise. These carried on throughout the pandemic, on Zooms and Teams platforms, providing the Forum members with an opportunity to reflect and learn – effectively, 'live time'. One could draw the analogy of building the aeroplane while in flight.

Multi-generational workforce

In terms of the multi-generational workforce, we have previously discussed the fact that Covid-19 may well have forced a new working paradigm; people who previously may have wanted to work flexibly and/or remotely had been less inclined to ask due to worrying about job security or how it may adversely affect their career, promotion or development opportunities. The pandemic has provided an opportunity for employees to illustrate they can be as productive, if not more so, while working from home. This also potentially saves employers premises costs and travelling expenses. For workers, they are afforded more time to be at home, the flexibility of being able to work when convenient, within reason of course, and having more disposable hours due to savings on commute times. Contrast that with younger people (and we generalize here) who may not have their own homes and share small spaces, equipment and Wi-Fi with others and who cannot work effectively from home, though clearly through no fault of their own. These cohorts may fully embrace a return to the workplace. In a turnaround, ironically, the 'traditional workplace' may be more suitable to younger cohorts due to the housing and/or financial situation they find themselves in. We see a future hybrid model in which younger people may substantially want to work from employer-provided premises and older workers the opposite.

Technology in the workplace

As we went into the first lockdown the use of remote working solutions was not widespread. For example, the Forum held every meeting in person, and so too did the majority of organizations. However, we have seen the burgeoning use of technology to find working solutions during the pandemic, and this is very unlikely to regress. With the introduction and widespread use of platforms like Teams and Zoom (and many others globally of course) we anticipate a huge uptake in the use of technology as we emerge from the pandemic. One of the main considerations for managers will be to control the availability of an online 24/7 workforce. The employees' right to disconnect becomes even more important; in other words, it's vital that people don't get techno stress. Employers will need to manage emails, phone calls and other access to their employees, so that people can have a family life and don't have to be online all the time. Techno stress is going to be an area to be well managed in order to keep the workforce productive and well. We have discussed the impact of presenteeism and leaveism behaviours previously and these have been well documented (CIPD, 2021). They have an enormous impact on wellbeing as well as performance and can also be the source of huge workplace stress. However, managed well they do not need to be on the radar. For example, we have seen some organizations already adopt Zoom-free Fridays and protected email times (see for example the French approach to weekend emails). That is, managers respect unsociable hours, weekends and when employees are on leave or unwell, when sending emails. Further, there is no expectation that employees will respond straight away.

Financial landscape

It is helpful to explain the trajectory prior to the pandemic. In terms of the economic position, on 3 June 2021 the Forum was fortunate to hear first-hand from Andy Haldane, the Chief Executive of the Royal Society of Arts and former Chief Economist of the Bank of England. Andy gave an overview of the economic state (of the UK) pre-Covid-19. He posited that the UK had been in a longstanding productivity crisis, with the economy effectively flatlining since the global financial crisis more than a decade previously. He reflected that the last period of similar static productivity would have been most likely the industrial revolution. Furthermore, he suggested that where productivity leads, pay usually follows and that there had been a lost decade of real pay rises for the average worker, running at 20–25 per cent below the path it should have been on pre-Covid.

Previous outbreaks

In terms of experience of dealing with similar health outbreaks, there have been numerous infectious disease outbreaks. These include diseases such as SARS (2003), H1N1 (2009), MERS (2012), Zika (2015) and Ebola (2013–16). However, and this in no way downplays these, but while they were all very significant epidemics and pandemics which resulted in huge loss of life, they were all contained when compared to Covid-19. This containment resulted in the global impact on society and the economy being relatively minimal, although we stress again that they were catastrophic for the populations they infected. By contrast, Coronavirus Disease 2019 (Covid-19) has been attributed to over 4 million deaths worldwide (out of over 190 million confirmed cases), making it one of the deadliest pandemics in history. This assessment of infection and death is believed to be grossly understated and at the time of writing it is still on the rampage in many countries throughout the world.

Reference

CIPD (2021) Health and Wellbeing at Work Survey 2021, https://www.cipd.co.uk/ Images/health-wellbeing-work-report-2021_tcm18-93541.pdf (archived at https://perma.cc/4NHZ-83AP)

02

Lockdown hits the UK

Covid-19 timeline

The pace and scale of the discovery and spread of Covid-19 was incredible. To illustrate, the World Health Organization (WHO) timeline records that on 31 December 2019, Wuhan Municipal Health Commission, China, reported a cluster of cases of pneumonia in Wuhan, Hubei Province. On 10 January 2020, WHO issued a comprehensive package of technical guidance online, with advice to all countries on how to detect, test and manage potential cases, based on what was known about the virus at the time. This guidance was based on experience with SARS and MERS and known modes of transmission. Just two days later, on 12 January 2020, China shared the genetic sequence of Covid-19. A day after that, Thailand reported the first case outside of China. On 30 January, WHO reported 7,818 cases globally in 18 countries outside China. On 11 March 2020, WHO declared a pandemic. Twelve days later, the UK went into its first lockdown.

'From this evening I must give the British people a very simple instruction – you must stay at home' – Rt Hon Boris Johnson MP.

On 23 March 2020, the UK Prime Minister made this announcement, which was to have a profound effect on the lives of all people living in the UK. The PM continued to outline the severity of the virus and the possible consequences of doing nothing:

… the coronavirus is the biggest threat this country has faced for decades – and this country is not alone. All over the world we are seeing the devastating impact of this invisible killer. And so tonight I want to update you on the latest steps we are taking to fight the disease and what you can do to help. And I want to begin by reminding you why the UK has been taking the approach that we have. Without a huge national effort to halt the growth of this virus, there will come a moment when no health service in the world could possibly cope, because there won't be enough ventilators, enough intensive care beds, enough doctors and nurses. And as we have seen elsewhere, in other countries that also have fantastic health care systems, that is the moment of real danger. To put it simply, if too many people become seriously unwell at one time, the NHS will be unable to handle it – meaning more people are likely to die, not just from coronavirus but from other illnesses as well. So, it's vital to slow the spread of the disease. Because that is the way we reduce the number of people needing hospital treatment at any one time, so we can protect the NHS's ability to cope – and save more lives. And that's why we have been asking people to stay at home during this pandemic. And though huge numbers are complying – and I thank you all – the time has now come for us all to do more (GOV.UK, 2020).

Lockdown

What then followed was a period of unprecedented limitations on the freedoms of people living in the UK – what became known as the lockdown. The lockdown initially legislated that people would only be allowed to leave their home for the following very limited purposes:

1 Shopping for basic necessities, as infrequently as possible.

2 One form of exercise a day – for example a run, walk, or cycle – alone or with members of your household.

3 Any medical need, to provide care or to help a vulnerable person.

4 Travelling to and from work, but only where this was absolutely necessary and could not be done from home.

Further, the following restrictions were also quickly put in place:

5 Meeting friends was prohibited.

6 Meeting family members who did not live in the same home was prohibited.

To facilitate this:

7 All shops selling non-essential goods were closed, including clothing and electronic stores and other premises including libraries, playgrounds and outdoor gyms, and places of worship.

8 Enforcement was put in place to stop all gatherings of more than two people in public – excluding people you live with.

9 All social events, including weddings, baptisms and other ceremonies, but excluding funerals, were stopped.

10 Parks were to remain open for exercise, but gatherings were to be dispersed.

New language

Another phenomenon that came along with the pandemic was a whole new gallery of words and phrases that were previously in little use, or were completely new:

Covid-19, Social Distancing, Flattening the Curve, Shielding, Isolating, Quarantine, Teams, Quaranteams, Zoom, Zoombombing, Working From Home (WFH), Self-Isolating, Lockdown, Key Workers, Jab, Second Jab, Track and Trace, Lateral Flow Test, PCR Test, Contact Tracer, Face Covering, Hand Gel, Reproduction R Number, Spike Protein, Field Hospital, Nightingale Hospital, Antibodies, Community Spread, Herd Immunity, Containment, Covid Toes, Long Covid, Fatality Rate, Hospitalizations, Immunocompromised, Mortality Rate, Pandemic, Personal Protective Equipment (PPE), Proning, Essential Worker, Furlough, SAGE, JCVI, Anti-vaxxer, Basic Necessities, Underlying Health Conditions, Vaccine, Ventilator, Induced Coma, Vulnerable Person, Barnard Castle, Asymptomatic, Containment Area, Epidemiology, Essential Business, Patient Zero, Physical Distancing, Super Spreader, Astra Zeneca, Oxford, Pfizer BioNTech, Variant, Moderna, Vaccine Passport, Quarantini, Staycation, New Normal, Level 0, Drive-thru Testing, Sanitizer, Pingdemic, Self-Isolate, Delta Variant, Bubbles and Stay at Home.

We are sure there are many more.

At the time of writing (Summer 2021) the UK is in the third wave of Covid-19, and organizations are once more trying to work out what a) normality is, and b) if they can viably return to making a living from what they were doing prior to the pandemic. The UK track and trace programme is causing chaos, with millions being told to isolate, meaning the majority of organizations are operating with skeletal staffing levels and thousands of school children have been sent home. Also, there is no guarantee in place that the relatively free movement being afforded at the present time will continue. The vaccine roll-out in the UK has been an incredible success for science, medical practice and logistics. However, there is a notable reluctance in young people to take up the vaccine and there are numerous variants of the virus being announced with alarming regularity; the future working environment is far from certain. What we are sure of, is that things will never be the same.

As lockdown was implemented, most organizations globally, we would suggest, were faced with the stark reality that most managers needed input and guidance on managing remote teams, and that employees needed input, guidance and equipment to transition to remote working – the largest forced working paradigm shift in the modern era.

The following chapters will give a fascinating insight into how a diverse range of organizations with workforces in the UK and overseas have reacted, adapted and strategized throughout the pandemic.

Reference

GOV.UK (2020) Address to the Nation on Coronavirus, https://www.gov.uk/government/speeches/pm-address-to-the-nation-on-coronavirus-23-march-2020 (archived at https://perma.cc/8HX3-JDPR)

How organizations responded to Covid-19

03

Policing the Covid-19 pandemic

ANDY RHODES

This section contains the reflections of a former Chief Constable, Andy Rhodes. The Chief Constable is the head of the Police Force in a particular area. The UK Government Home Office is responsible for policing and governs 43 police forces in England and Wales. The National Police Chiefs Council (NPCC) has a number of business areas to coordinate and aligns activity among the 43 forces. Andy leads on the Wellbeing portfolio for the NPCC and is also the Director of the National Police Wellbeing Service. There are also Chief Constables in charge of the Police Service of Northern Ireland and Scotland, as well as a number of non-Home Office forces (e.g. British Transport Police, Civil Nuclear Constabulary). Andy talks of how emotions matter in a crisis such as Covid-19. He was tasked with contributing to the Covid-19 response for policing (Gold Group) as the pandemic hit and developed. At the time of writing the UK is in the third stage of lockdown and vaccines have been delivered to 'at high risk' groups.

Lancashire Constabulary is the ninth largest of the 43 forces in England and Wales, with a workforce of 5,500 people serving a population of around 1.4 million. On an average day Lancashire Police typically receive 1,000 999 calls, 3,000 non-emergency calls and record 500 crimes. It's been my home since birth and my workplace for 29 years, so I know the places and the people pretty well, I think!

Policing can be an incredibly unpredictable affair; nothing is ever as simple as it first seems. To that extent, there is a need to build a resilient delivery model that can withstand a crisis or a series of incidents. When demand outstrips supply, like with any business, policing priorities are to focus on the basic 'core' services – pick the 999 phone calls up quickly, get to the emergency jobs fast and investigate the most serious crimes.

Moving through the ranks I have been privileged to learn the theory and practice of crisis management. I take pride in regularly practising them in my own force and also on national events or operations. There is something about the pace, complexity and pressure of a crisis that appeals to me. This is perhaps because the normal frustrations born out of working in a hierarchical culture quickly fall away. It can be empowering, liberating and exciting. The police family do not always thrive when things are routine, boring and predictable and so I know I'm not the only one who thinks this way. Although many crisis events and operations can last for several days, weeks or even months, nothing we have experienced before has endured to the extent of Covid-19. My reflections on 2020 are drawn from my role as Chief Constable in Lancashire as well as my role supporting the National Gold Group with responsibility for Personal Protective Equipment (PPE), Testing and Policy.

I often reflect by asking myself the following:

- Under pressure, have we in policing been able to sustain the commitment, the focus and the attention in terms of our mission to provide world-class wellbeing support for our people?

- Most importantly, what have we learnt that can be used to prepare us for the next time?

- Have we perhaps finally witnessed a fundamental shift in organizational thinking to one where we understand that what happens to us outside of work affects what happens to us in it?

VUCA: when the abnormal becomes normal

As human beings we are wonderfully unique, necessitating a personalized, artisan relationship with the place where we spend so much of our lives. The current world we live in is increasingly volatile, uncertain, complicated and ambiguous. Described as VUCA (Casey, 2014), how do we respond when the abnormal becomes normal?

Much has been written about the 'new normal', but unless you are Jeff Bezos or Elon Musk it can feel out of reach for the vast majority of leaders, who are just trying to keep the plates spinning. VUCA is a useful term to describe the way the pandemic feels most days and can help leadership teams shift their mindset from either a) pretending they are in control when they are not, or b) losing their sense of agency while descending into a state of learnt helplessness.

Working out what you can control, what you can influence and what you have to accept, is useful reframing for the leader or manager. It can help them feel more comfortable with not knowing what is happening next. I decided to start with VUCA because my experience of Covid-19 has brought the concept into sharp reality, moving it from an idea to something that has actually become 'normal'. In my experience, it is common to forget that a crisis is an emotional experience because under pressure, systems, structures and protocols dominate the airtime. This leaves little room or inclination to ask simple questions, such as 'how are people feeling and how will they feel as a result of this decision?'

Nobody has ever asked this question in any crisis event I have been involved with. To understand the emotional experience of a crisis we first need to understand some basic fundamentals about our brains and how we process threats.

At a personal level we are not supposed to exist in a state of VUCA for too long. This is because the human brain was not designed to spend all day in fight or flight. We generally crave certainty, clarity, facts, routine and if we don't get them we can suffer from anxiety and stress. Neuroscience teaches us that anything we perceive as a threat will elicit these survival responses. In his book, *Resilient* (2018), Rick Hanson describes how a fear of the unknown can create 'paper tiger paranoia'.

In his book *Why Zebras Don't Get Ulcers* (2004), Robert Sapolsky shines a light on the damage existing in a state of perpetual 'fight or flight' has on the human condition when compared to a wild animal, in this case a zebra. Zebras have exactly the same neurological survival instinct as humans and it generally stands them in good stead when faced with an immediate threat, such as a lion in the bushes. In milliseconds messages fire through the zebra's body, triggering instinctive responses to escape from the threat. That is assuming zebras never decide to hang about and fight with the lions of course! And so do our brains. But the difference is what happens next. Zebras very quickly return to a normal relaxed state, with heart rates, blood pressure and cortisol levels reducing. Zebras do not continue to ruminate and worry about what they could have done better, or whether it really is or isn't a threat according to the scientist they've just listened to on the five o'clock briefing! You can see where I'm going with this? Humans just aren't cut out to live in a state of perpetual VUCA, and by recognizing this we are better equipped to start doing some practical things to help them cope. The paradigm shift we need to make in a crisis is to see work as an opportunity to make our lives better, not worse.

It is my deeply held belief that Covid-19 has proven work to be a much-needed 'port in the storm' for those of us who have been fortunate enough to keep working.

The plan is… there is no plan

Very few organizations will have constructed a people plan capable of dealing with Covid-19. Even the most determined executive teams can often struggle to embed wellbeing as a strategic endeavour when things are quiet. By strategic I mean a whole organization and a whole life approach. Yes, we have got business continuity plans, operational contingency 'E' plans for every eventuality. But, let's be honest, nobody saw this coming, and from day one we have been scrambling to get ahead of the curve. Covid-19 has proven the case for investing in a strategic and long-term wellbeing plan. Further, I will set out why I think it is the differentiator and a priority as we start to prepare for the next crisis.

Firstly, a good wellbeing plan will bring together the needs of the business, the evidence base and employee voice to create a shared purpose, grounded in the lived experience of the people nearest to the work. You will have worked out what people care about and how much belief they have in their leadership team. There will be well-established channels of engagement whirring away 24/7 that are used to listen and respond to people's needs – not just an annual staff survey. A culture of healthy conflict rather than false harmony will be developing, and deference will no longer be a barrier to people feeling confident to raise concerns about organizational issues such as risk, fairness and respect. In a crisis the last thing the Executive need is to be told everything is fine. They need to hear the truth and hear it fast!

Secondly, a good plan will have already brought together the people with the right skills, experience and passion you are going to need to work through the daily, hourly challenges created by a pandemic. You will have a team – even if it is in the loosest sense of the word – and therefore you will be able to rapidly gain a broader range of perspectives. This, as well as the connections back into vital areas such as HR policy, occupational health and staff networks.

Finally, a plan can be adapted. If you do not have a plan you are starting from scratch rather than going through a rapid review of existing priorities and planned activity. The vast majority of our plan was still relevant, and it is important to maintain momentum in the face of a crisis. So, our main task was to create capacity and capability for new work specific to Covid-19, meaning some things had to be put on hold. This is an important consideration and was particularly relevant 10 months into the pandemic. It may be ok to temporarily overload your people to get through a peak in demand, but you will need to reduce their other commitments very quickly or they will burn out and lose faith in you.

So, if you had a plan going into Covid-19 then you won't have been scrambling as much as if you did not have one. Either way, when you are in the midst of a crisis and everyone is looking to you for reassurance and direction, I find it useful to frame my approach around something more strategic than a delivery plan. It helps me stay focused on what really matters, and it forms the thread of a narrative I use to engage my senior leadership teams and the wider workforce. For Covid-19 I have used Rick Hanson's description of three human needs, although others may have their own preference. However, this has worked for me. It helps us remember the 'why?' question.

Human needs

I have chosen to follow Rick Hanson's advice and framed the organizational challenge of Covid-19 in relation to his proposition that to thrive we have three 'human needs' which are fundamental to a 'good life'. I think they suit the threat of a global pandemic quite nicely. According to him, our three human needs are:

1 Safety: Covid-19 threatens our physical, psychological and financial safety.

2 Connectedness: Covid-19 has reduced our connectedness and increased isolation.

3 Purpose: Covid-19 has the potential to distract us from the organization's purpose.

Safety

When we do not feel physically and psychologically safe, our basic human needs are not met, thus causing anxiety and distress. Maslow's hierarchy of needs starts with shelter and food, realizing if these things are not in place, self-actualization is several steps too far. Initially, when Covid-19 struck we saw a range of threats to our safety, ranging from job security to a fear that our NHS system would collapse under the pressure, removing our psychological safety net. For the first time we heard our people talking about feeling frightened for their loved ones as a result of a work-related risk. In policing this has never happened before to my knowledge. Our people willingly place themselves in harm's way all the time, but Covid-19 was different. 'What are you going to do to prevent me from taking this home to my family?' I was asked in the first week.

Placing oneself in harm's way is discretionary. That is to say, nobody can order you to do it (Hesketh and Cooper, 2019). Discretionary effort is the lifeblood of policing and we should never take it for granted. It can (and will) be withdrawn when people feel they are not being cared for by their leaders, their organization and society. In my organization, we have been on a journey for several years, determined to increase 'employee voice', and only recently have we started to see tangible, measurable benefits. We have a multitude of well-established channels to engage with our people, and so we heard this voice immediately. If you go into a crisis like Covid-19 with a culture where deference filters out bad news, the voices of the people nearest the work will be silenced, only to emerge when trust and confidence have been lost. You will be in recovery mode rather than being on the front foot.

Our people demanded PPE, hand sanitiser and evidence of deliberate leadership thought being applied to the risks they were facing. What I saw, as alluded to earlier, was an unleashing of energy being applied to managing the crisis. An incredible buzz as teams cranked into action to lead the partnership response to Covid-19, including new legislation to translate into consistent practice and the humanitarian effort. The wheel started to spin very fast and the focus on the people was crowded out. There is only so much airtime in a planning meeting and if the main challenge is setting up a temporary mortuary for 1,000 bodies, who is going to raise their hand and ask about the impact of school closures on workforce resilience or where we can source hand sanitiser? Answer – nobody!

Yet, for our people, these things were the most important and when asked they will say represented physical and practical evidence that the bosses cared about them. By taking the people issues outside of the operational meetings, it enabled us to apply sufficient time, thought and commitment into the daily (often last minute) problems created by Covid-19. We were able to listen, address and respond on a more personalized level than ever before. No more sheep dipping with a 'one size fits all' HR policy. Covid-19 has taught us so much more about the uniqueness of each other's lives. Our HR teams have reached down the line 24/7 to support line managers and individuals seeking help and advice, while also ensuring risk assessments were reviewed regularly. Long may this last after the crisis!

Connectedness

Does anyone remember when 'social distancing' was not even a phrase? No doubt it has already made its way into the *Oxford English Dictionary* because it became so familiar in 2020. Apart from the fact it is impossible to maintain distance (socially or not) as an operational police officer, I have been using this human need to stay focused on something I think we are only just starting to see the true impact of. Celine Schillinger (www.weneedsocial. com) reminds us that work is simply a network of social connections, many of which the executive are unaware of. Further, even if they do know about them, they are unlikely to be invited into them.

For most people, connection is fundamental to leading a 'good life' and while all too often we may take it for granted, I think it is the one human need Covid-19 has affected the most. Much is written and spoken about compassionate leadership and the 'empathy era', yet how does one convey these sought-after traits when all around you there is chaos?

Firstly, we need more than words. There are some technical, detailed actions peculiar to a pandemic, which must be taken to provide flexibility, guidance and support for people who are forced to reduce their connection to loved ones and work colleagues. In a high-stress environment, social gatherings are often a vital antidote, a coping mechanism to help people process traumatic events. It is not just a team pizza, it is far more than that, and the limitations needed for social distancing will have a psychological impact, one which is possibly even greater than the physical risks of Covid-19.

Covid-19 has exposed many more people to traumatic events, such as losing a loved one, being unable to visit care homes or hold a proper funeral. Vital elements of any grieving process have been denied. When I refer to work as a 'port in a storm' I'm thinking about the social connections, bonds and strength we gain from being with others, particularly through hard times. A recent ONS survey I saw asked what we had missed most about work after retirement. Sadly, the number one answer was 'nothing' but the second answer was 'the people'. That is because Celine is right; work is social and throughout Covid-19 the mental health benefits for those of us who have been fortunate enough to keep coming into work may well prove to be our saviour. I hope so.

Purpose

In our most recent staff survey, people reported 90 per cent + clarity of purpose. Keeping people safe is a high-level, straightforward purpose enshrined in law through a sworn attestation with a magistrate. This is conducted from when police officers join their force. Of course, purpose is far more nuanced and often a deeply personal issue influenced by a range of different aspects of life – organizations do not have a monopoly on purpose, and we all reserve the right to change our purpose in response to the ebb and flow of life.

In March 2020, when Covid-19 first broke, the engagement team started to develop a specific strategy to inform and reassure our people on an almost hourly basis if necessary. This was essential, given we were given no notice of policy changes. As such we were continually reacting to daily government announcements that our people were watching in real time. The plan, and our subsequent engagement messaging, were based on the understanding there would be a shift in the priorities of our people even if the organizational priorities were all about business continuity. When we face a personal health crisis we stop thinking about less important things, zoning in on survival. We recognized Covid-19 would have a similar effect on many of our people, particularly if they had health-related vulnerabilities themselves, or with loved ones.

March 2020 was not the time to trot out the organizational purpose, unless it could be integrated into how people were feeling about their own vulnerabilities. Every message we gave out blended our organizational purpose of keeping people safe (as a critical service leading the local response phase), to the individual purpose of keeping ourselves and therefore our loved ones safe. Linking the organizational purpose to 'what I really care about right now... this very second' creates an emotional connection between our work and our personal lives.

We know many police officers and staff think about 'keeping people safe' as being about people other than themselves, mainly because the majority of people we engage with are either vulnerable due to circumstance or random victims. Not so with Covid-19 – it is indiscriminate and random, which is why it frightens us, I think. Covid-19 has created a personal VUCA dynamic. Purpose is intrinsic and as such invisible to the naked eye. The emotions generated by a crisis are also invisible, requiring us to suspend judgement, listen and empathize so that we can tune into shifting priorities and walk in the shoes of others.

What next?

There are two organizational priorities moving forward. Firstly, we have to look backwards and learn from the experience so that we can assess what worked, in particular how resilient we have been at an organizational and individual level. We then need to test this learning as soon as possible because we need to prepare for the next crisis.

Secondly, we must draw on the evidence we need to understand the impact of the crisis on our workforce mental health, motivation and performance. The National Police Wellbeing Service conducted its first-ever workforce survey towards the end of 2019 and its second survey at the turn of 2020. Comprising 23,000 responses, the results surprised many of us. Overall, people reported improvements in key areas proven to improve wellbeing. Emotional energy is up, sleep has slightly improved, psychological detachment has significantly improved and so has feeling valued by our colleagues and our organization. Physical wellbeing has deteriorated along with feeling valued by the public. Accepting that police officers and staff score higher than the general working population in most of these areas, ie the baseline is too high already, these are fascinating results worthy of further analysis. For example, psychological detachment is proven to be vital for recovery – so what has happened in 2020 to improve this? We must use data like the survey to improve wellbeing when there isn't a crisis.

By opening up a conversation with our people now, we can start to assess their needs and tune in our organizational wellbeing support. This will undoubtedly help them recover so that our organizations can emerge from the global pandemic more connected, more empathic and more inclusive.

References

Casey, G W (2014) Leading in a VUCA world, *Fortune*, **169**(5), p 75

Hanson, R (2018) *Resilient: Find your inner strength*, Penguin Random House, London

Hesketh, I and Cooper, C (2019) Wellbeing at Work: How to design, implement and evaluate an effective strategy, Kogan Page, London

Sapolsky, R M (2004) *Why Zebras Don't Get Ulcers*, Times Books, New York

04

Fujitsu

Information technology and the Covid-19 pandemic

KELLY METCALF
This section contains a case study from Kelly Metcalf. Kelly is the head of diversity, inclusion and wellbeing for Northern and Western Europe at Fujitsu Limited, a Japanese multinational information technology equipment and services company headquartered in Tokyo. *Fortune* named Fujitsu as one of the world's most admired companies and a Global 500 company.

During the Covid-19 pandemic, Fujitsu's priority has been to sustain the positive wellbeing of all employees, while delivering our customer commitments.

At the time of writing, Fujitsu is the seventh-largest IT services provider globally and the largest in Japan. We use our experience and the power of information and communications technology to shape the future of society with our customers. With 130,000 people globally, and nearly 7,000 in the UK supporting customers across all sectors and industries, our people are at the heart of everything we do.

As the extraordinary events of the Covid-19 pandemic took hold during 2020, it was essential to us to ensure we supported all our employees as much as possible. Within the space of one week, we moved the majority of our workforce (around 90 per cent) to work fully from home. Our technical capabilities helped us to achieve that seamlessly, but we know that technology alone does not help people to work effectively: it's technology, combined with great people focus that achieves this. So, we centred our efforts on the human impact of this transition. Recognizing and supporting the unique individual circumstances of each person, proactively supporting managers to help their teams through this change journey, and demonstrating genuine and authentic leadership commitment to support wellbeing, all became our focus areas.

All of this has enabled us to continue supporting our customers effectively. We helped move tens of thousands of people to remote working, safely and securely, enabling our customers to continue providing vital services. For example, by moving 45,000 more people to remote working, a major bank could provide uninterrupted service, so they could help those in financial need. We tripled remote connections by 275 per cent for the UK Armed Forces to help keep everyone safe and gave back by using overseas engineers to fill the gap in support when other suppliers were unavailable. We helped keep the lights on in over 10 million UK homes by enabling 18,000 staff, including entire contact centre teams, to work from home at one of the largest energy companies, which was seamless, rapid and secure. We helped the UK government support victims of domestic abuse with technology critical to the cause during difficult times, and the Home Secretary publicly recognized our contribution. We helped support vulnerable customers in financial need by deploying hundreds of robots to support rapid processing of requests for mortgage holidays. We kept people connected and in a single month at the start of lockdown, we deployed 90 per cent more instances of Microsoft Teams, allowing more people than ever to collaborate virtually.

In this case study I will highlight the key themes underpinning our support for employees.

The essential role of line managers

From day one of the shift to primary remote working, managers have been encouraged to check in with their people even more regularly than usual – ideally daily. The aim of this is to check in with how people are feeling; how they are finding their working arrangements and any personal circumstances that may be impacting them. We have very publicly focused on these as 'check-ins', not about checking up on people. We trust our people to deliver their output. Our UK people management population is around 700 people. We held weekly webcasts providing these managers with the latest guidance, policy changes, health and safety updates and ensured all of these included 'wellbeing chats' – practical content they could use in team check-ins. Over and above information-sharing sessions they started to build the management community, tackling the same goal – maintaining and developing connection with people who we now see much less.

Our leadership team complemented these with regular business updates and focused sessions for their teams, with more regular communications and demonstrating genuine care for their people. Our leaders took care to share their own experiences of the pandemic, how they're working differently, the struggles this gave them personally, and set the tone for an open culture to talk about our wellbeing. 'Shape your leadership' virtual learning sessions were available to all managers, helping them to learn more about practical ways to better engage remote teams, support employees' mental health, have courageous conversations and provide personal support for our management community during the additional pressures they faced; something that can easily be neglected. All of these sessions were packed with takeaway insights and practice tips and received excellent feedback from participants.

Conscious inclusion

We recognized very quickly that the pandemic has affected each person in Fujitsu differently. Health concerns for those in vulnerable groups, worries for loved ones, additional caring responsibilities in the home, lack of an optimal home working location, living in shared accommodation... every person had their own story and set of circumstances. By emphasizing that each person is an individual, we encouraged managers to understand everyone's unique circumstances and agree the right working pattern or tailored practical support to help. For many, this included many more flexible working arrangements than we have ever seen in the past – especially during the time of school closures. This also included practical support such as additional work equipment in the home; financial contribution to the purchase of a desk; provision of an office-quality chair; an extra five days' paid leave for carers of children and other dependents; and more paid volunteering time for those involved in local charity support. We launched a 'Home Workers Assessment' as a framework for managers to proactively review the efficacy of someone's homework space and to consider the impact of homeworking on each person's physical, social and mental wellbeing. We used the feedback from these assessments to identify any additional adjustments or support, including prioritized return to the office where appropriate or seeking alternative work arrangements for anyone experiencing domestic abuse.

As a result of this personalized support, people were able to continue working productively. Further, during the time of the period, we saw a 7 per cent increase in employees reporting a sense of effective team collaboration. We also saw a 6 per cent increase in people understanding how their work contributes to Fujitsu (Dec 2019 to Sep 2020 employee survey results).

In addition to the essential role of people managers and managers being encouraged to check in with their people regularly, we also regularly checked the sentiment of all employees through pulse surveys. Designed to understand how supported employees felt and where we needed to focus more attention, we learnt a lot from this feedback. In the early days of the pandemic, we learnt that the experience of colleagues working in an office location or doing mobile work was less favourable than their colleagues based at home. As a result, we put in place tailored support for this group – targeted communications to keep everyone fully informed of support and health and safety measures especially. We also became more sensitive in overall messages to employees, ensuring that any communications were inclusive for everyone – not only targeted at the majority based at home. As a result, we saw a convergence in experience between remote and site-based workers during April to September 2020, of 9 points when surveying their overall experience of Fujitsu at that time.

Flexibility by default

At Fujitsu, we trust our people to deliver. We believe that looking after our people leads to them looking after our customers and Fujitsu. We have accommodated thousands of informal flexible working arrangements, agreed between manager and employee, to help people manage their work and life priorities. We took the decision not to furlough anyone, instead asking those who had less work to do because of the pandemic to work on internal 'business advantage' programmes. This includes a group of people working on a digital accessibility programme, to help us become even more inclusive in how we use technology to support our colleagues with disabilities.

For people who were vulnerable due to health conditions, we adjusted their role where necessary, to enable them to work from home. If this was not possible, we provided sick pay at full pay for the entire time spent shielding, with no impact on their sick pay entitlements.

This flexibility extends beyond working hours and location to supporting employees to use their quieter times productively. Our Talent team created a 'one-stop shop' for all employees to access learning and development in support of their career development. We also made a wealth of free external courses available to employees and others in their household: to date these have been accessed by over 6,000 users.

As a Responsible Business, we are committed to supporting society and local communities, so we increased the number of paid volunteering days available to employees and promoted opportunities for people to virtually volunteer. We also hosted a 'Virtual STEM' (science, technology, engineering and maths) activity week to inspire colleagues' 7–11-year-old children towards careers in STEM and intentionally timed this during the summer holidays to offer support for parents.

The positive impact that this flexibility has had is demonstrated in employees' feedback, with 73 per cent saying they feel able to effectively manage their work-life balance in September 2020, compared to 68 per cent in December 2019.

An open mental health culture

It is important to us that our culture supports positive mental wellbeing and normalizes talking about mental health at work. We are signatories of the Mental Health at Work Commitment and beyond celebrating individual dates in the wellbeing calendar, such as Mental Health Awareness Week, we have a clear leadership voice on the topic. Our leaders share their own experiences of mental health, we share regular employee stories, and all of this helps to normalize talking about mental health at work and helps everyone to feel comfortable acknowledging when they're not ok and need additional support.

We run a regular series of events, with different things happening weekly and for employees to join: webcasts with colleagues and leaders sharing their personal experiences of mental health, 'Sustaining your wellbeing' interactive sessions, 'Developing emotional resilience' events, as well as access for everyone to the support of our Employee Assistance Programme and Best Doctors Mental Health Referral Service.

Building conscious inclusion into how we sustain mental health, we have also targeted support for employees with different experiences. For example, clearly recognizing the circumstances of those experiencing loneliness due to isolation, targeted mental health support for our diverse communities, led by our Diversity and Inclusion networks, and events focused on men's mental health.

Our regular managers' calls often focus on mental health-related topics, steps managers can put in place to avoid burnout, e-presenteeism, and to ensure managers know our people 'as people' so that through their regular check-ins they can spot any behaviour changes or signs suggesting people may need additional support.

Our Mental Health First Aiders have been available to all employees and run drop-in sessions for anyone needing additional support.

We proactively encourage healthy work practices in communications to all employees: reminding people to schedule regular breaks during the work day and time away from their screen together with encouragement to get outside every day; avoiding setting meetings at times that are unsuitable for colleagues with caring responsibilities; scheduling calls for 25 or 45 minutes, instead of 30 or 60 to allow natural breaks instead of back-to-back calls; and designating 'walking' meetings. Through our 'Remote Working' collaboration site, webcasts, team meetings and employee consultation groups, we encouraged everyone to share examples of how they were sustaining their wellbeing, to motivate others to do the same. And we introduced 'Work your Way' time – an hour per week for people to book as non-work time to do whatever they choose, away from their screens, in support of their own wellbeing.

Proud to be Fujitsu

Recognizing that positivity and feeling connected to a bigger purpose can contribute to employee wellbeing, we created a 'Proud to be Fujitsu' collaboration site, in which we shared positive stories of the services that Fujitsu employees continued to provide to help our customers continue to deliver their essential work for society. We encouraged our people to be proud of each other. Since Mental Health Awareness Week in May 2020, employees have contributed to a virtual Kindness Wall where they were encouraged to share messages of thanks/stories of kindness they received from their colleagues. This wall was available from May–November 2020 and culminated in celebrating some of the inspiring stories shared on World Kindness Day, November 2020. All of these activities helped to reinforce a sense of team, community and peer support among our people. In addition, sharing positive messages with employees of how their work has contributed to the essential work of many of our customers has helped to reinforce this collective sense of purpose.

Closer connections with our leaders

While remote working poses many challenges, it has also been an incredible leveller. Our leadership team has been more visible to all employees than ever before. Where previously interaction with the regional leadership team may have been through quarterly in-person 'Town Hall' meetings, our people have had the opportunity to hear from our leaders in their own homes, to 'see' them more regularly, and to hear their personal stories of life in lockdown and experience of the pandemic. Experiencing our leaders encountering some of the simple things that affect everyone when working at home. Interruptions from family members or hearing a barking dog all contribute to seeing leaders as real people that are in the same boat as everyone else. This openness and authenticity, combined with our leaders encouraging all of their teams to be open about their personal circumstances, has created an environment of genuine care for each other.

And there's no going back

While we continue to recognize and be sensitive to the challenges that the pandemic has posed for everyone, each in different ways, we have seen the best of Fujitsu through the past months. Despite these challenges many people have also found a better work-life balance, with reduced stress and travelling times contributing to greater wellbeing and productive output. Seventy-nine per cent of people feel well supported by Fujitsu, 83 per cent feel supported by their managers, and all of this manifests in an 11-point increase in employee engagement (December 2019 to July 2020).

We are actively involving employees in planning the future beyond Covid-19. From employee survey results in September 2020, 85 per cent of people told us they want to be able to flex their time between home and office in the future. This feedback, combined with insight from employee Focus Groups, which have brought together diverse groups of employees in different roles, levels and business areas, informs our plans to sustain more flexible working in the future. A theme across all of this feedback is that people tell us they value Fujitsu's central focus on people, inclusion and wellbeing during the pandemic and want this to continue in the future.

This tells us that we've been doing some things right and we remain committed to sustaining greater flexibility in both where and when people work in the future. This is Fujitsu's promise to sustain the 'Work Life Shift' for both our customers and ourselves in the future. In addition to the wellbeing benefits this will bring, we are certain that this will help us to attract, retain and progress the careers of more diverse talent for the future. So it's clear to us... there's no going back!

05

Consultancy

The elusive origin of strength in a crisis

BRUCE DAISLEY

This section contains reflections from Bruce Daisley. Bruce is a workplace culture consultant and the author of *The Joy of Work*. His previous role was that of European Vice President for Twitter and creator of number one business podcast, *Eat Sleep Work Repeat*. He is currently writing a book about resilience and how we can find it.

During the summer of 2020 I found myself in Lebanon. My partner is from Beirut, so we were delighted to escape from the shores of Britain to make a trip back to the city for a week's holiday. Little did I know it was out of the frying pan into the fire. When I say fire, I mean it. It might have escaped your memory but on 4 August 2020 Beirut played host to the biggest ever peacetime explosion in a city.

We found ourselves three miles away as a series of explosions at the capital's port shook Beirut and its surrounding districts. Our own building rocked for a full minute; it was 6.0 earthquake. Thirty seconds into the shaking our windows blew in and the screeching inhalation of the explosion sucked all of the air from the apartment. It was like nothing I'd ever heard before.

The next day news reports from around the world broadcast live from the rubble of Beirut's port. The BBC struck a pretty characteristic tone. They reminded viewers that 'the Lebanese are famed for their resilience'. One correspondent for the *New York Times* filled in the gaps in the same way: 'Anyone who knows Lebanon has heard this: the Lebanese are resilient.'

But the people around me didn't feel like that. People were broken, upset, distraught. Aside from Covid-19, the Lebanese had just battled through 12 months that had seen their banks collapse and their life's savings vaporize. And now this. Half of the city's windows seemed to have been shattered. While the wind had a chemical bite to it, the sound of daytime was the scratchy tinkle of glass being swept from the streets.

Resilience was the most desired character trait of 2020. We were all expected to show it. But like a lost bank card, if we didn't have it to hand, it wasn't immediately obvious where we'd find it. I was intrigued to see how the Lebanese people had been famed for having supplies of it in droves. But to my own eye they didn't seem so much resilient as broken, and weary in their defeat. They only went on because, 'well, what else can we do?'

Twenty-four hours after the blast, it was another news outlet that captured a local person expressing closer to what I had seen first-hand: 'I really thought I'd seen everything in this godforsaken country. How much more are we supposed to take? If I hear one more person referring to us as "resilient", I will lose it. F*** resilience. We don't want to be resilient. We just want to live!' I reflected on when I had heard use of the word 'resilience'. One of the times was on a radio discussion I'd had with Robert Peston that year. Peston was talking in the midst of the A level grades fiasco that had occurred in the aftermath of Covid-19 when poorer kids had seen their exam results being knocked like skittles versus their teachers' projections. Our screens had been filled with despondent, panicked youths. Peston had adopted a sympathetic tone but had added, 'The truth is that young people need to be more resilient.'

What do these two things have in common?

Well, it seems we tend to use the word resilience to describe what we expect from the victims of a system. When we want them to dust themselves down and get on with things. I remember being given a book in my first job. It was a bestseller by Ken Blanchard called *The One Minute Manager*. To brutally abbreviate what was already a pretty brief text, *The One Minute Manager* uses effective delegation to get a job off a leader's To Do list and empower someone else to do it. A good manager should offload the distraction of unexpected events by ensuring someone else deals with them.

Resilience seems to be advice from the One-Minute Counsellor. 'Your exam results are disastrous?' Ok, you have my sympathy, but you need to be resilient. 'Your city has blown up at a time when you have no money to rebuild?' Ok, but let's see some of that Big Boy Resilience you're so famous for because we've got another person to help in 30 seconds. I've spoken to people who have had resilience training, who have been on resilience courses, who have read books on it and time and time again after this support they are left wondering if their feeling of defeat is simply their own fault.

That's not to say that there aren't routes into a hardy, robust response. In fact, this book contains wonderful evidence of exactly those responses, but rather sometimes the R word isn't, in itself, helpful.

Resilience can be a simple word that we use because it is easier for us to expect a response from the victim of a misfortune than for the system to question how we got here. Whether you are Robert Peston or the *New York Times*, demanding resilience allows for the attention to move on; the responsibility is transferred to the victim to sort themselves out. The One-Minute Counsellor gave you your moment but now we've got to move on; remember to be more resilient and I'm sure things will be ok.

Of course, the flaw in this is when we look at the incidence of misfortune. It tends not to be the successful who are at the receiving end of the injustices of life. Rather, our economic and social systems tend to impact the lives of the Have Nots rather more than the Haves. We've got into the habit of thinking that it's ok to have the Have Nots learn to cope.

I spent my time when I returned from Beirut trying to get to the bottom of where we can find this inner strength. Where our own fortitude lies. The myth of resilience is that it's a trait that individuals can exhibit on demand. That any one individual has a magical super-power that allows them to survive adversity. And the myth is that if you don't show it, it is because you didn't want it enough. A victim ends up feeling like they are to blame for their own misfortune.

So, I wanted to look into how we can actually be stronger. I'm going to avoid using the word resilience because it is overused. So, let us call it fortitude. And here's what I discovered.

The truth is that fortitude is most commonly a collective response that we exhibit when we feel supported by others around us. This is really relevant for everyone reading this, because it will inform how your team, your organization and even your company can respond to challenges.

Control, identity and community

There are three critical components of fortitude: control, identity and community. Firstly control. Why is control important for fortitude? There is pretty good evidence that when we have control over our circumstances, we feel more able to soldier on. Researchers have shown that nurses who work long shifts feel less burned out when they choose to work longer. It is almost like the act of choosing to go on gives us more strength to do so.

Even an illusion of control can help. Social scientists have done a series of grim experiments on animals. One especially bad one saw rats immobilized in a tank of water; the little things had been injected with Botox. The rats who were given a piece of wood to chew on, giving themselves some way to mitigate the way they were feeling, were less stressed (Ono et al, 2012). Even with drowning rats, when they have control, they feel more able to carry on. You might recognize this? Whether it is the rats or the nurses, when we feel like we are in charge it changes our perspective on how to persist. So, one of the critical components of fortitude is control.

Secondly, I mentioned that one of the important components of fortitude is identity. Back in the ancient realms of social science there was a very famous experiment that was known as the Stanford

Prison Experiment. You will have heard of this. It found that a group of students when given roles of guards or prisoners very quickly became assimilated into those roles and behaved in shocking ways. Sadly, there is plenty of reason to believe that the researchers involved deliberately subverted the results, so 15 years ago the BBC asked two social scientists to try to replicate it.

In fact, the results were very different. They found that some things were true. The roles for the participants were chosen at random. The guards who, of course, knew that the experiment was being shown on the BBC, became very conscious of their role and were a little ashamed of the fact they were giving orders on screen. The prisoners felt a glorious sense of connection with each other. Initially they were delighted to be on a pretend Naughty Step and then in the face of the guards' embarrassed disassociation with each other the prisoners' own self-esteem grew to fill the void. Their pride in their free-spirited identity expanded, their chests puffed to delight in the mischief they set about creating.

As the experiment went on, the researchers found that a lot of what was happening was measurable in the stress levels and happiness of the participants. To make it worse, not all of the guards felt the same level of self-consciousness. So those who dwelled in an embarrassed awkwardness were in a daily conflict with those who wanted to be stricter with the convicts. On average, during the course of the experiment, the stress levels of the guards went up as their lack of faith in their own identity and any shared values with their fellow guards went down.

On the other hand, the identity of the prisoners showed a real improvement. They formed something of a Prisoners' Union, instituting a strike for better privileges and developing a strong bond with each other. As time went on their anxiety levels dropped even further, and they reported feeling genuinely happy despite their restricted liberty. On every possible measure the prisoners were happier than the guards. One of them described himself as 'happy as a pig in shit'.

All in all, this is not how the experiment was meant to work. But we see repeatedly that when we feel connected and proud of our identity it makes us feel stronger. By the end of the experiment the prisoners reported feeling more able to cope than the guards. Effectively, the prisoners had shown more fortitude, more resilience in a stressful situation.

The important thing about identity is that we often look around us and ask, not necessarily if we like the individuals we see, but about ourselves in the reflections of the people we see. Seeing those around us, it invites us to ask ourselves, 'who am I?'

As some of the leading researchers in this field – not least Alex Haslam and Stephen Reicher, who ran the BBC Prison experiment – have asserted, a substantial part of our sense of self and who we think we are derives from our group memberships and our sense of social identity.

And that takes us on nicely to the third vital ingredient for fortitude, and that is community. When we found ourselves in the midst of the pandemic a lot of us hadn't been in our colleagues' presence for months. Some of the cues of human connection had gone missing from our day-to-day life. There is very good evidence that the more we feel part of something bigger than ourselves, the more it actually impacts our mental and physical health. In other words, being connected makes us stronger. The way that one leading expert in this field explains it, for a long time health professionals have spent a lot of time categorizing the taxonomy of different mental health disorders, but it seems like the lack of social connection is the common denominator that underpins all of these areas (Haslam, 2015).

Rather than asking if you have this disorder or that disorder, the question is more like, 'are you disconnected from a sense of community?'

One longitudinal study vividly showed this (Cruwys et al, 2013). They tried to predict the likelihood of patients who developed depression relapsing back into it. If you didn't previously belong to any social group, your risk of relapse was really high – 41 per cent. However, the more social groups you reported being part of, the lower your risk of relapse. And it is not just depression. Researchers have found that this same strength is exhibited by patients who are recovering from heart attacks and strokes. Strangely, then, the best way we can get people to recover from major illness is to give them a better social connection with friends. When we are looking for the keys to fortitude, being connected to others seems to be a pretty formidable one.

Control, identity and community. But when we hear people demand a resilient response, we don't hear discussion of these themes. When our bosses ask employees to be resilient, maybe they need to be asking, 'How can we make our team members feel more able to make decisions? How can we make them feel more respected for the unique approach they bring to their work? How can we make them feel more supported by colleagues?'

Clearly this matters a lot in the modern workplace. In the course of the Covid-19 lockdowns, engagement levels among workers initially went up massively as many people reported feeling motivated by being in crisis mode. As time went on there was a growing sense that things weren't as good. We've found that if colleagues felt unable to control their calendar, they felt uneasy and anxious.

Identity has always been an important part of our lives, but one of the ways that we have developed our identity is by being around others, and the absence of that has been a significant issue. Screens do not always help here. I worked for 12 years at YouTube and Twitter. One of the things we learnt was that when people feel a strong affinity with someone else, then connecting through screens can bond them. But when we connect via a screen with a person who doesn't share our opinion, there can be conflict. Making sure that people feel their identity is respected and listened to is a really important action we all need to take right now.

Finally, community. When we feel connected to others it makes us stronger. We see this in the health evidence and in the response of those around us to the challenges we face. I found myself intrigued as to why some organizations were responding to the challenges of the Covid-19 era by hiring Community Managers. When I went to speak to these people, I was struck by their assessment of the task facing them. They told me that their job was to make their colleagues transcend their circumstances of home working and make them feel connected to each other, to use elements of identity and community to ensure they didn't feel emotionally isolated.

It makes an intriguing contrast with what we have been told. When we have heard talk about resilience before it has often been seen as a personal expectation; the resilience of the people of Lebanon or the A level students was something we looked to others to show. In fact, the lesson for all of us is that fortitude is something that we need to collectively create the conditions for.

We don't just step and exhibit strength of character, we are given the support that enables us to experience it. Maybe coronavirus gave us a timely opportunity to reconsider how we think about resilience?

References

Cruwys, T et al (2013) Social group memberships protect against future depression, alleviate depression symptoms and prevent depression relapse, *Social Science & Medicine*, **98**, December, pp 179–86

Haslam, A (2015) Social identity and the new psychology of mental health. Speaking at 2015 Division of Clinical Psychology annual conference in Glasgow, https://www.youtube.com/watch?v=TWWZd8lrraw&ab_channel=The BritishPsychologicalSociety (archived at https://perma.cc/Z89P-NCR8)

Ono, Y et al (2012) Active coping with stress suppresses glucose metabolism in the rat hypothalamus, *Stress*, **12** (2) pp 207–17

06

Universities

Blurring edges – leading teams and institutions in Covid-19

SIR CHRIS HUSBANDS
This section contains an account from Sir Chris Husbands, who is the Vice-Chancellor of Sheffield Hallam University.

> *Leadership is a difficult practice personally because it almost always requires you to make a challenging adaptation yourself. What makes adaptation complicated is that it involves deciding what is so essential that it must be preserved going forward and what of all that you value can be left behind. Those are hard choices because they involve both protecting what is most important to you and bidding adieu to something you previously held dear: a relationship, a value, an idea, an image of yourself (Heifetz, 1995).*

My university, Sheffield Hallam, is one of the largest in the United Kingdom. It occupies four sites in Sheffield: a city-centre campus, a suburban campus, a research and development campus in east Sheffield and a large sports centre in the north of the city. In total, the university educates 32,000 students and employs 4,500 staff. It is the size of a small town, and with much the same proud sense of identity and community. Our students come from across the United Kingdom and from more than 100 countries, but roughly half grew up and were educated in the Sheffield city region. It is a university proud of its place. Before lockdown, as the Vice-Chancellor – chief executive – of the university, one of my most important routines was to spend time out and about among our students and our staff, listening hard to their experiences of learning, teaching, studying, researching, supporting the institution. I invariably picked up useful insights into the tough strategic questions my job involved my team and me in handling: getting out and about around the estate, listening and looking, was one of the most valuable things I did. Visibility as a leader is a powerful instrument in the leadership toolkit. It is what the leadership guru Ron Heifetz calls 'getting on the balcony': that position from which leaders can 'see' their organization and the landscape beyond the organization, but, equally, can be seen by their organization.

In March 2020 the 'balcony' was ripped away. Within 48 hours the university was required to pivot to largely remote operation across almost all of its functions. In some areas we had seen this coming for some time; in others we had been determined to maintain a face-to-face offer for as long as we could. Just a few days before the injunction to all organizations to work remotely, I'd spent time on a Saturday in one of our libraries. I talked to the students – about 100 of them, working away in study carrels – about why they were working in the library on that Saturday morning. I learnt more about students with weak broadband connections at home, no good or safe place to work, noisy children, the requirement to use specialist software and so on. Within days, my library teams were required to find creative solutions to those challenges. Right across the university, I was invariably impressed by the solutions our teaching, technical and support teams put in place: this was an organization moving quickly in the face of unprecedented challenge. I remain humbled by the range, scale and effectiveness of what my colleagues did over the weeks and months following March 2020. But I was also aware of something else: in remote working, I could not so obviously climb 'onto the balcony'. I could not see and be seen. My sense of where my organization 'was' began to shift. Whereas I 'knew' where the university started and ended – the walls and fences around the campuses – it now had a much more diffuse set of boundaries. The campus, in a phrase we began to use more and more, now 'extended' into nearly 40,000 homes. I began to think hard about what this meant for leaders and for leadership.

Leadership, of course, is about people. It's about how we inspire, enthuse, engage, persuade, support, cajole, sometimes direct people. It's about how we envisage, describe, shape, mobilize and sustain change in institutions to make a better future. It's about how we imagine, communicate and map transformation. It is above all about interactions: between the present and the future, between what is and what could be, between mind and heart, between leaders and led. Leadership can never be done in the abstract. It gains traction in context. There are – and airport bookstalls would be much less thickly populated if there weren't – general principles about vision, about strategy, about change, about challenge – but leadership becomes real when it is grounded in context and place and institution. The outstandingly successful English cricket captain, and later trained psychotherapist, Mike Brearley, in his, for me, compelling book, *The Art of Captaincy*, tells the story of a 'lionkeeper at the Dublin Zoo called Mr Flood, who was remarkable in that over the years he had bred many lion cubs but never lost one. When asked his secret, he replied, "No two lions are alike"' (Brearley, 1985). Leadership is a conversation between a vision of future possibility and the present realities. It involves shaping a compelling narrative about what might be, and then mobilizing intellectual, emotional and psychological resources to map the route forward. It involves a dialogue between possibilities and constraint, between imagination and reality. Challenges between what is and what might be or what needs to be can 'only be addressed through changes in people's priorities, beliefs, habits, and loyalties' (Heifetz, 1995).

Covid-19, of course, presented itself initially as a major incident that required crisis management. In most conventional crises, the focus of crisis management is on the immediate, the need to be returned to normal as soon as possible. Almost all leaders have experience of this sort of crisis management, which arises from the unexpected incident in part of the organization. For myself, a few weeks before the Covid-19 lockdown, a small group of 12 students on a field trip overseas were held up at gunpoint by a gang of criminals. They were robbed, and half of them had their passports stolen. For a week, a crisis management team worked long hours to address the dimensions of the situation: the traumatized students; their deeply concerned, and in some cases angry, families; the complex liaison between consulates and local police forces – one of the students whose passport had been stolen was not a UK national. Within a few days, all were safely home. This was crisis management as most leaders know it: something untoward, unexpected happens and there's a need to address the urgent situation, while elsewhere the life of the organization proceeds.

Covid-19 was different. It involved at least three things simultaneously. First, it involved an instant disruption to the routines not of one part of the organization but of the entire operating and business model – an instant, and overwhelming disruption, generating organizational, logistical, educational, managerial and emotional challenges. Secondly, it involved preparation for an unknown, untested, untried and challenging mode of operation for an apparently indefinite period. This was initially a three-week lockdown, then extended, and, for all practical purposes, extended again, so that by the time I write this, we have been operating in remote mode for some eight months. The 'immediate' was not simply immediate but open-ended, exacerbating staff and student anxieties. And third, in this case crisis management would not involve a rapid, or even phased return to 'normal', but to what McKinsey called a 'next normal' (McKinsey, 2020), in which a combination of continued long-term social distancing, new social norms, practices learnt during lockdown and massive economic and social dislocation required radical change, if unconditional change for institutions. This was a challenge not simply for leaders but for leadership. It was a profound disruption to the conversation between the future and the present, between the possible and the real. We are all of us, whatever and wherever we lead, out of our customary habitat: the world of the face-to-face contact with an organization, the world of the task group and the committee, the one-to-one and the planning meeting, the roundtable budget conversation, the corridor conversation and the walk around.

Educational institutions are made up of people: student populations, staff teams. But while that's true, it's not, immediately how we think of universities: we think of them as places. They have a location;

their buildings – high quality or low quality, geared well for the sorts of teaching that take place in them – define them. They have a physical footprint, demarcated by fences and walls and, increasingly, we see security arrangements that control access to them. There are laboratories and studios, workshops and classrooms, lecture halls and seminar rooms. A frequent tool for governments seeking to direct investment into education improvement is to invest in new buildings; a frequent complaint from teaching staff and leadership teams is the quality of the buildings they have to work in. Educational institutions are places, they exist in places, and they exist for places. So, there is an obvious question in the wake of the Covid-19 crisis: what is the nature of an institution when its relationship to its physical location and form is loosened, when the operation of the organization moves outside the physical constraints of place? Where are the boundaries of space when the university reaches into the homes, spare rooms, bedrooms, kitchens of 40,000 people?

This relaxation of the relationship to place and space is an automatic consequence of the transition to remote working. Internal organizational geographies collapse. Classes can be assembled in virtual locations; teams can be drawn together at the click of a switch. Equally, of course, the reverse applies: some students – and some staff – cannot be located. These are enormous challenges for operation in remote mode, loosening the assumptions customarily made about the way teaching, learning and space work together, about the relationship, indeed, between teaching and learning, between teacher and learner. The loosening had already begun to happen. The rapid development of mobile technologies and their increasing deployment in learning, the accelerating use of social media as a teaching tool – these had begun to loosen the hold of place. But for most institutions, information technologies had augmented rather than replaced space; despite the enormous investment in learning technologies over the past 40 years, basic assumptions about the deployment and organization of space in institutions had barely shifted, and the key building block of institutions – the classroom – has barely shifted. The adaptation forced by the Covid-19 crisis has unleashed a widespread set of questions about the operation of educational institutions as place. Once assessment, for example, has migrated online on one occasion, there is no strong argument for ever moving it back into large examination halls.

This transition may be relatively temporary. It may be that we will look back on the era of the Covid-19 crisis as a blip, and that we will find ourselves reverting to pre-crisis ways of thinking about institutions as places, in places and for places. But this feels unlikely for several reasons. First of all, thinking about place was already shifting. By and large, crises accelerate developments already in-flight. Secondly, the sheer pace of technological adoption during the crisis has opened up a wider sense of possibilities which have, as I have already suggested, shifted the way in which individuals and groups are comfortable working. Finally, there is a clear sense across organizations and society that the consequences of what is in essence a society-wide shutdown of 'normal' is shifting wider assumptions: the 'next' normal will not be what was 'normal'.

Conventional operating models are being upended. Even if many elements of previous practices re-assert themselves for most institutions, operating models will need to adapt in different ways: to continued social distancing, to changed financial exigencies, to the impacts of technologies on teaching, learning and staff interaction, to different commuting and travel-to-work patterns. The balance between different modes of teaching, forms of engagement and ways of working is changing rapidly and is unlikely to disappear overnight, if at all. They all feed into strategic and organizational delivery questions. Suddenly we have a digital learning lab at scale that is millions strong. Some detect an opportunity here; at the very least this will turbo-charge investment and developments in educational technology. *Forbes* quotes Matt Greenfield, Managing Partner of Rethink Education, an edtech venture firm:

> ... there are hundreds of millions of students in China experimenting with various forms of online learning. We have tens of millions in the US, and many more around the world... A lot of institutions are experimenting and it's going to be hard to go back (McCauley, 2020).

A common theme of my own conversations with institutional leaders is that this process of redesign, of thinking through operational models, is challenging – and becomes more challenging as time goes on. That in itself creates a danger that any return to face-to-face delivery within currently vacated buildings loses the potential for radical change. There is a tension between the potential of the moment and the ability of institutions to reform themselves after change experiences: the 'old normal' may reassert itself over attempts to reimagine a 'different normal'. The tension between holding onto the 'old' and sustaining what has been learnt in the 'new' is fraught.

In all of this, the principle of self-authorization that has emerged within institutions applies to the institutions as well: leading change without seeking permission to initiate change. Crises are destabilizing; they undermine established ways of working, but they also enable institutions to find their inner strength and, certainly for confident institutions, to set a bold course for the future. It turns out that the source of the quotation 'never let a good crisis go to waste' is contested – Churchill, Saul Alinsky and Rahm Emmanuel are all cited as its originators – but the precept is well established. Crises threaten but they also open up possibilities for those confident enough to seize them, willing to use them not simply to prepare for the future but to define it; not simply to respond but to reshape, redefining direction on the basis of core underlying values and overarching educational purposes. The task is to find ways to shuttle between constraint and possibility, empowering organizations to reshape operations within an overarching purpose.

Self-authorization of change, and the opportunities to reimagine the workings and place of the organization are the great prizes here, but they are not enacted, of course, in a vacuum. Institutions exist in relation to place, but they also exist in relation to each other. Competition and competitive advantage have been lodged into the workings of the sector. Institutional purpose is also about institutional distinctiveness, and institutional distinctiveness is a way of differentiation from other, neighbouring institutions. One of the features of the immediate response to Covid-19 was a reassertion of common purpose. In sector after sector, the nation needed not just 'this' or 'that' institution but institutions, and for institutions to think about the common good. The differences between schools, between colleges, between universities suddenly became less pertinent than the similarities between them. The urgency of the need to respond placed a premium on sharing experiences and swapping information. This was the immediate experience of crisis. It's not clear how enduring this sense of a shared response will, or can be. It's easy to see how the emergence from crisis and particularly the emergence from crisis into a financially constrained environment could tip sectors back into destructive competition in which it is every institution for itself. Typically, governments do gratitude very badly: there will be poor recollection of collective purpose. Competitive ethos could reassert itself. If so, the delineations of the post-crisis world will look more like the pre-crisis world, a world of competitive edge, of putting the institution first. If there is a belief in common purpose, it will still take brave and committed leadership to put learners and their needs ahead of the institution and its priorities. This will require leaders who can move quickly from handling the institutional response to crisis to thinking hard not just about what their own institution needs to look like and do, but what the sector as a whole needs to look like and do. It will need confident and articulate relational, as well as institutional leadership.

References

Brearley, M (1985) *The Art of Captaincy*, Coronet, p 199

Heifetz, R A (1995) *The Practice of Adaptive Leadership: Tools and tactics for changing your organization and the world*, Harvard University Press

McCauley, A (2020) How Covid-19 could shift the college business model: 'It's hard to go back', *Forbes Magazine*, https://www.forbes.com/sites/alisonmccauley/2020/04/09/how-covid-19-could-shift-the-college-business-model/ (archived at https://perma.cc/B9QS-F97M)

McKinsey and Company (2020) Beyond coronavirus: The path to the next normal, https://www.mckinsey.com/industries/healthcare-systems-and-services/our-insights/beyond-coronavirus-the-path-to-the-next-normal (archived at https://perma.cc/7Z4Y-8UWL)

07

NHS Employers

The National Health Service and the Covid-19 pandemic

JENNIFER GARDNER
This chapter is written by Jennifer Gardner, who is the Assistant Director at NHS Employers.

The NHS is made up of 1.3 million staff who provide dedicated and compassionate support and care for patients. For them to do this effectively, it is essential that the safety and wellbeing of individuals and teams is supported and prioritized. This was the case before the pandemic, in the already-stretched, under-resourced, understaffed and underfunded NHS where, despite this, NHS organizations were doing their best and providing fantastic examples of robust programmes prioritizing the wellbeing of staff.

NHS Employers is the employers' organization for the NHS in England. We help employers to develop a sustainable workforce, improve staff experience, and be the best employers they can be. Our practical resources and expert insights help make sense of current and emerging healthcare issues, to keep employers up to date with the latest thinking, and ensure they are informed and equipped to support the NHS workforce. We generate opportunities to share knowledge and actively seek the views of workforce leaders to make sure their voice is front and centre of health policy and practice. We also lead the national collective relationships with trade unions on behalf of the NHS and the Secretary of State for Health and Social Care.

People are the heart of our NHS and are key to its resilience. Their skills, knowledge, compassion and dedication have been evident throughout the pandemic. Yet, a year of intensive pressure, preceded by a challenging winter, has taken its toll on them, both physically and mentally.

According to the latest figures, staff vacancies still stand at over 87,200, and sickness absence rates continue to be higher than normal, even while the NHS is expected to do more than ever before. NHS organizations continue to do everything they can to look after and protect their people but are collectively concerned about the wellbeing of their staff and that many may leave the service if too much is expected of them in the aftermath of the pandemic.

Adapting and innovating during Covid-19

Covid-19 has shone a light on and exacerbated many of the workforce challenges faced by the NHS and has placed significant burden on the workforce, bringing the experience of staff into sharp focus.

The pandemic has uncovered and reinforced the urgency and importance of the health and wellbeing agenda, highlighting lessons to learn from and build on, including health inequalities and the need to get the basics right for all.

Despite the relentless pressure of Covid-19, we have seen real innovation and transformational change in organizations where they have prioritized staff experience focusing on safety, wellbeing, engagement, flexible and agile working practices, and inclusivity in a collaborative, joined-up way.

Taking a joined-up approach

Rather than addressing the different elements of staff experience in silos, a joined-up approach can lead to a more inclusive and comprehensive strategy that drives the wider workforce agenda and leads to a collaborative cultural shift.

Collaboration has been key to achieving successful staff experience outcomes at pace, enabling greater capability and effect when working together across disciplines, listening, sharing, and learning as part of a shared vision and commitment to look after and support our staff.

Collaboration was a key principle at Imperial College Healthcare NHS Trust, where a 30-person multi-disciplinary reference group was established, representing different ethnicities, ages, bandings, teams and departments across the trust. Building on the expertise in the organization and leaning into the groundswell of energy from staff to support wellbeing, enabled the trust to utilize key skills and expertise and take a staff-led approach, so the final support offer was made for NHS staff, by NHS staff.

A three-phase model was implemented to support staff wellbeing through the critical phase (focused on supporting immediate practical, physiological, and psychological needs to help keep staff healthy, happy and safe), the aftermath phase (focused on support for staff experiencing trauma, moral distress and PTSD) and the recovery phase of the pandemic (focused on re-engagement back into the role, the future and longer-term impact of the pandemic on staff, and ongoing wellbeing support). The pandemic has helped integrate the wellbeing of the workforce into the culture, values and behaviours of the organization and fostered a determination to continue this approach.

The pandemic has, for many, put a real focus on staff wellbeing and has accelerated the need for collaborative, inclusive action.

Promoting a culture of wellbeing

Investing in and embedding a culture of wellbeing was a priority for many NHS organizations prior to the pandemic. However, when there are competing pressures and demands and limited finance, staff wellbeing can become 'a nice to do' rather than a necessity, but these are often the times when it is most in need of focus. Covid-19 has already starkly highlighted the impact of trauma, burnout, and rising sickness absence levels on the NHS workforce.

A pitfall of wellbeing programmes that has also been highlighted due to the pandemic is the need to ensure programmes and interventions tackle the root cause of staff wellbeing issues and not the symptoms. This requires a move away from an output-driven agenda, such as focusing solely on sickness absence, to an input-driven agenda concentrating on values, positive leadership behaviours, and outcomes for sustainable, long-term effective staff experience cultures.

The pandemic highlighted the need for organizations to reprioritize and focus on the basic needs of staff. For example, ensuring that staff have access to hydration and nutrition; the ability to take breaks; time out to reset when they need it; somewhere to sleep when they can't go home because they are protecting their families and loved ones; and enabling them to be safe and to feel able to look after themselves and their colleagues first.

Ensuring NHS organizations provide the right support to protect the health, safety and wellbeing of the NHS has never been more critical. The basics must be provided as the foundation, and programmes built from there.

Royal Devon and Exeter NHS Foundation Trust developed a comprehensive mental health support offer for staff, building on existing services, to ensure staff could access the support they needed.

Gaining insight through staff engagement

Many NHS trusts have approached the challenges of engaging with staff during Covid-19 by implementing a range of innovative, creative, and thoughtful methods of gathering staff feedback and addressing the issues raised.

The trusts that achieved successful responses were flexible in their approaches and sought to develop and deepen staff engagement in their organizations.

To inform and shape the wellbeing strategy in preparation for a second wave, Wrightington, Wigan and Leigh Teaching Hospital NHS Foundation Trust refreshed its local survey to include 16 questions focusing on how the trust had supported staff through the pandemic.

Sussex Partnership NHS Foundation Trust launched a 'Learning for the Future' project at the outset of the pandemic to capture live feedback from staff about the changes introduced during Covid-19. The project generated a total of 2,500 survey responses on issues including wellbeing, remote working and decision making. This feedback directly informed the development of a 'Learning for the Future' framework; a set of principles and expectations to inform team discussions and decisions about future working practices.

Blackpool Teaching Hospitals NHS Foundation Trust created a rainbow installation at its main site as a place for patients and staff to thank people for their efforts during Covid-19. The rainbow helped sustain staff morale, create a sense of unity and shared purpose, and ultimately came to be a highly visible symbol of staff appreciation.

Birmingham and Solihull Mental Health NHS Foundation Trust (BSMHFT) used the Idea Drop virtual crowdsourcing platform to share and develop ideas about staff wellbeing and understand how services might change for the better in the post-pandemic world.

Prioritizing equality, diversity and inclusion

One of the defining factors of the pandemic has been the disproportionate impact it has had on staff from minority groups, including LGBTQ+ staff, those with disabilities, and black and minority ethnic communities (BME).

While it has highlighted inequalities and compounded the emotional, mental and physical health impacts for many of our frontline colleagues, for many trusts it has also encouraged a more inclusive approach to supporting staff.

At Mersey Care NHS Foundation Trust, the respect and civility team aimed to create a positive working environment to support staff during the pandemic. One of the ways they did this was by running virtual versions of previously successful events. For example, following the success of their Odd Socks campaigns in November 2018 and 2019 that aimed to raise awareness of bullying, the team got staff involved in a virtual anti-bullying event to raise the profile and support for Anti-Bullying Week across the trust and social media.

The team shared their message of kindness across the organization through the Be Kind in Lockdown civility and respect initiative that was implemented in May 2020 in response to the pandemic. Slogans for the campaign were Be Kind, Civility Saves Lives and I Will Speak Up. This video features members from across the respect and civility team speaking about their own experiences working during Covid-19 and how they have been supporting themselves and colleagues. The trust also offers two free modules of online training, which highlights the importance of behaviours to equip staff with the necessary confidence and tools to speak up if they witness something they think is not right. The training gives examples of best practices, which aim to reinforce areas where staff are already doing well.

The Covid-19 vulnerable health clinics instigated by East Sussex Healthcare NHS Trust provided a safe space for supportive conversations, which were also used to support the risk assessment process to create more inclusive conversations around wellbeing and ensure BME staff knew what support was available to them.

At Birmingham and Solihull Mental Health NHS Foundation Trust (BSMHFT), using Microsoft Teams has driven an increase in engagement with employee networks. After a powerful and emotional session following the death of George Floyd, the trust covered inequalities and racism in several of its weekly Listen Up Live question-and-answer events with the chief executive. The trust reported that the sharing and support offered in the network sessions and at virtual Schwartz Rounds has so far been as effective as previous face-to-face events.

Supporting new ways of working

A major shift for many NHS trusts has been the requirement for staff to work from home and the need to adopt digital technology into their daily working lives.

Changes to working practices were also created by the need to redeploy staff away from their usual roles, staff being required to shield, or staff returning to work after a period of absence. This presented new challenges to supporting the experience of staff working remotely.

To help tackle the immediate issue of people feeling isolated and disconnected while working remotely, Birmingham and Solihull Mental Health NHS Foundation Trust (BSMHFT) created some new engagement opportunities following a virtual crowdsourcing exercise. These included a network group for staff who were shielding and a Stories to Connect virtual event that allowed remote working staff to jointly reflect on their experiences through poems and stories at the end of each day.

After resolving the challenges of making sure people had the equipment and skills to work from home, Hertfordshire Partnership University NHS Foundation Trust (HPUFT) created the HPUFT Working Differently Guiding Principles. The principles were designed to help staff navigate the challenges created by working remotely and encourage a supportive and compassionate conversation. They included reminders that staff were not simply working from home, but were 'at home, during a crisis, trying to work', and that success would not be measured the way it used to be.

HPUFT also held virtual coffee mornings for staff who were shielding to help them stay connected and in touch with their colleagues. Parents were supported to work flexibly as they managed childcare responsibilities during school closures. New training in the form of bite-sized workshops helped managers support and manage their teams remotely, with a focus on compassionate leadership and wellbeing. Live-streamed Q&A sessions with the trust's chief executive and board were attended by hundreds of staff. All the activities contributed to 95 per cent of staff saying HPUFT cared about their wellbeing in the July 2020 staff survey, which was a 7 per cent increase from the year before.

Reaching staff through good communication

At the start of the pandemic, with so much to communicate in a short space of time, it became essential that key information was communicated in a timely and digestible way. This was even more challenging when trying to communicate with a staff population who were already under enormous pressure and often working even longer hours.

Getting messages to harder-to-reach staff groups also became a bigger challenge as the fast-changing situation and high stakes meant everyone needed to have certain information.

Trusts used a range of activities to deliver their messages, from digital Q&A sessions to floor walking, alongside existing communications channels.

Sussex Partnership NHS Foundation Trust (SPFT) created a variety of channels to communicate with staff, including an app with a dedicated wellbeing section, podcasts, blogs and webinars. The diversity of channels allowed staff to engage with information in the way that suited them best.

Leading through a crisis

Visible leadership at all levels has been a critical success factor throughout the Covid-19 pandemic and has had a significant impact on staff experience.

Those in leadership roles have been squeezed by demands from below and above, compounded by requirements to manage new ways of working, redeployed staff and mounting demands, as well as overall support and guidance at a time when the service was facing an unknown situation that was developing at pace.

Line managers were called on to lead their teams in challenging, uncertain and unfamiliar environments.

North East London NHS Foundation Trust recognized it was crucial that the additional impact on leaders was acknowledged and extra support provided. It piloted a project offering support through

30-minute resilience-building phone calls to line managers and leaders every three weeks, in addition to the usual support available. The calls focused on increasing resilience, self-care, emotional support, reframing of challenges, building positive relationships and helping their teams do the same. The pilot was evaluated by a pre- and post-evaluation focusing on specific quality of life metrics, which showed that the participants' scores for coping with current stresses improved, as did scores on sleep.

Eight per cent of managers who participated said they were listened to and understood. During the second wave of the pandemic the support was rolled out to line managers in another service area and the outcomes were even more positive, as improvements had been made to the process based on the initial pilot.

The NHS Health and Wellbeing Framework and Health Education England's Staff and Learners' Mental Wellbeing Commission Report both recommended the need for checking in with staff and training for managers to support wellbeing conversations. The NHS People Plan requires that:

> From September 2020, every member of the NHS should have a health and wellbeing conversation and develop a personalized plan. These conversations may fit within an appraisal, job plan or one-to-one line management discussion, and should be reviewed at least annually. As part of this conversation, line managers will be expected to discuss the individual's health and wellbeing, and any flexible working requirements, as well as equality, diversity and inclusion. From October 2020, employers should ensure that all new starters have a health and wellbeing induction.

The implementation of health and wellbeing conversations for all NHS staff identified actions in the NHS People Plan, and the continued application of NHS Employers' eight elements to support effective health and wellbeing strategies, will continue to support NHS organizations to embed health and wellbeing into the culture of an organization.

In conclusion, there remain many uncertainties about Covid-19 and one that will remain for some time to come is what impact this will have on NHS staff in the longer term. To get something different in the future we must do something different, behave differently and think differently, with staff safety and wellbeing at the heart of what we do, because without our NHS people there would be no health-care. Staff and their teams are our biggest asset. We must put them first and enable and support them to do the same.

The NHS is committed to keeping staff at the heart of what we do and making sure that we share and learn from our own experiences and the experiences of others to sustain this focus and enable all staff in all organizations to be safe, well and to thrive.

The examples in this chapter demonstrate that where organizations prioritize the health and wellbeing of their staff, they can not only survive a crisis, but come out of it stronger than before.

08

Microsoft

Managing wellbeing in a crisis – a Microsoft view

KAREN SANCTO

Before sharing the journey that wellbeing at Microsoft UK has taken over the course of 2020, it is important to set the scene.

Microsoft UK supports a wide demographic of around 4,500 employees, across all age groups, genders, races and personal circumstances. Our employees have the autonomy to work flexibly, in the office, at home or at customer sites. As part of a global corporation, with many UK employees reporting to managers based outside in another geography, we already had a remotely supported and agile workforce; a business that had the tools to move quickly to home working as the need arose.

Deeply embedded within the company are two expectations: high impact and a growth mindset. This is a broad commitment to understanding and delivering against customer needs, fully embracing learning and supporting and building success with others not just as individuals. Within this cultural framework there are also high expectations of resilience both from the business and from individuals themselves.

To help them deliver against their goals, employees are supported through extensive employee benefits and wellbeing resources, including learning, physical and emotional support, onsite fitness centres, onsite clinicians and gym memberships.

All these elements resulted in both strengths and challenges – particularly caused by the constraints imposed during a health pandemic and when rapid change is required.

At Microsoft UK, the wellbeing team focused on managing these challenges by addressing the following:

- effective, empathetic communication;
- putting wellbeing first;
- creating practical pandemic policies.

Communication

With the developing pandemic situation, we felt that employees needed transparency. They needed to understand what the impact was for them in terms of their daily schedule, place of work, ongoing customer engagements, as well as priorities and expectations from the business. We also wanted to emphasize the importance of wellbeing – and to reassure employees that their health and wellbeing and that of their family came first. It was important for them to feel empowered to make decisions to prioritize this.

HR partnered with leaders and managers, supporting them in the 'model, coach, care' framework. We encouraged them to practise a healthy work/life balance, coaching employees through more regular check-ins either at individual or team level, focusing on wellbeing and prioritization of work. Managers are talking to employees about how to manage their own individual circumstances, providing care through listening, signposting to wellbeing support, and agreeing flexible working patterns.

In our communication channels across the UK and the wider global regions, leaders and employees were sharing both inspiring stories and realistic accounts of how they were managing this unprecedented situation.

Communication within teams became an intentional activity to replace the previous opportunities to 'catch up' in the office over coffee or lunch. We aimed to raise morale through online activities –

either formally within team meetings or informally through social connections. The essence of community was evident, as the employee resource groups and other social teams increased their level of activity and outreach.

We were conscious of being sensitive in the frequency of our communications with employees. Where workloads were increasing at home and at work, we wanted to be mindful of asking employees to consume more information and attend more connections, and that they should take action to self-care. We ensured all our events were recorded so employees could listen on demand at their convenience. We also provided a 'menu' of suggested activities, so employees didn't feel they were missing out by not attending everything on offer.

Wellbeing

Microsoft UK offers a robust programme of services, resources and activity to support employees:

- a flexible benefits package;
- community network and employee resource groups;
- a volunteering and giving programme;
- a comprehensive suite of learning resources.

Complementing these resources is an established Wellbeing Strategy – supporting physical, emotional and financial wellbeing. With the partnership of an external health provider and a dedicated Wellbeing Manager, we provide onsite services at our larger office sites, with clinical services ranging from a GP, physiologist, physiotherapist, cognitive behavioural therapist and complementary therapy (acupuncture, reflexology and massage).

A number of these services can be accessed remotely – either directly or via an equivalent service. For example, employees could visit a GP on site or access a virtual GP via an app on their phone. Employees can also have an annual health assessment from one of the other UK sites as the wellbeing team schedules roadshows for these and other events (including the flu vaccination programme).

With Covid-19 forcing our offices to close, we had the challenge of delivering a virtual wellbeing service at a time when employees needed this support more than ever.

Our providers quickly adapted their services to ensure we guaranteed support for critical healthcare and continued to deliver our programme of proactive wellbeing. They offered virtual health assessments and coaching, online fitness apps, plus an ever-growing library of articles and recorded content. The wellbeing team programmed panel discussions and expert presentations on a range of topics. These included mental health during Covid-19, caring for others, coping with bereavement and exercises to prevent musculoskeletal problems. In addition, we worked with our financial benefit providers to ensure information was readily available for those who needed support in managing their cashflow and investments.

Our operational teams shifted their focus from managing health and safety in the workplace to supporting health and safety at home. Vital to employees' physical wellbeing was ensuring that appropriate furniture and technical support were available – with chairs and monitors being couriered across the UK.

To assist with clear employee guidance, we pulled together all our resources into a comprehensive guide to Wellbeing and Working from Home – to support both employees and managers. Headings included 'health and wellbeing of you and your family', 'financial wellbeing', 'successful remote working', and a list of resources to support productivity. Included in the guide were a list of frequently asked questions on policies, how to manage benefits and finances, how to access the wellbeing services and top tips to care for employee wellbeing during this time of lockdown and worry. We prompted employees with the importance of connection and a reminder of the employee resource groups.

As a result of our increased promotion of the wellbeing services and the clear messaging from leaders on the priority for self-care, we saw engagement and utilization levels of our wellbeing resources and services increase. There was a rise in those seeking support from our employee assistance programme, citing anxiety, relationships and parenting among the top concerns.

Practical policy changes

With the first lockdown, which saw schools and nurseries closed, both in the UK and across the world, it became evident that our existing care-giving leave policy would be inadequate to support parents at this time.

With a commitment to flexibility and empathy, Microsoft rolled out a global policy to support parents – offering up to 12 weeks of Paid Pandemic School and Childcare Closure Leave. Employees were given the flexibility to take it in blocks of weeks, days, or a day or week as appropriate. We saw this ease the tension of conflicting priorities between work and children.

As holidays and foreign vacations were postponed or refunded, we saw annual leave requests cancelled. This raised a concern that employees weren't taking breaks from work and having the rest they needed. Leaders and managers encouraged employees to use their leave for the benefit of their health, promoting the power of short breaks, long weekends and staycations to support employee wellbeing.

Questions were raised among employees and leaders about the impact of Covid-19 on the future of the workplace. We saw the launch of the Hybrid Workplace Flexibility Guide – a step-by-step guide to working where and when you work best.

Conclusion

The pandemic has accelerated transformation in many areas. We've seen how leaders can use technology to effectively communicate messages at scale – to reassure employees of the importance of wellbeing first and foremost. We've seen managers remotely support their employees during tough times, themselves being supported by leaders as they model their own management of this challenging situation. We've seen employees and communities come together, through virtual meeting rooms and online chat. We've also seen growth in the use of our accessibility tools through this digital transformation.

With our wellbeing services moving from in-person to virtual delivery, we've achieved a level of inclusiveness that might have taken months or years to achieve, as we can now support employees regardless of their ability to visit an onsite clinic. While our commitment to providing onsite services will continue, for every service we offer, we now have the ability to provide a virtual alternative – in combination, a truly accessible offer.

The impact of having formal guidance to support employees in how they balance work and home, to empower them to make choices to support their circumstances and individual wellbeing, is such a powerful and welcome consequence of the pandemic.

Looking ahead, with the agility we have for responding to a crisis such as Covid-19, through modelling our growth mindset and continuing to listen to our employees – from what works to what they really value during times such as these – I feel assured that we can support our employees throughout future challenges.

09

Construction

Maintaining the health and wellbeing of Mace colleagues throughout Covid-19

KERRIE SMITH

'Safety first – going home safe and well' is one of our core business values; this means that at Mace, we place health, safety and wellbeing at the heart of everything that we do to prioritize our greatest asset – our colleagues. Living and breathing this value has never been more important than during the Covid-19 pandemic.

Ensuring the health, safety and wellbeing of Mace colleagues while maintaining business resilience has taken collective, collaborative and innovative effort across all areas of the business. The collaboration and team spirit that we are all in it together as 'One Mace' has enabled us to become a stronger, more resilient and more connected business, recognizing that with change comes opportunity.

Reflecting on our new business purpose to 'redefine the boundaries of ambition', to thrive, not just survive, off the back of the pandemic, many of our departments, projects and teams had to redefine, and in some cases reinvent what they do and how they do it, at pace.

We have seen the impact of the efforts in 2020 in this year's engagement and wellbeing survey delivered in partnership with Robertson Cooper. The results tell us how, despite a difficult year of adversity and uncertainty, our Mace colleagues are more resilient, have more conversations for wellbeing, feel more purposeful and feel more connected and supported than they did in 2019.

At the Group level, all results in comparison to 2019 are better or have stayed the same, which is testament to the hard work that has collectively gone in to keeping our colleagues safe and well and is something that we as a business are very proud of. That's not to say there aren't areas to address going forward, but overall, a promising set of results following a challenging year for all.

Protecting our people

At Mace we have Gold, Silver and Bronze resilience groups that were formed to shape our response to Covid-19 and to manage the crisis on a global level.

A number of core workstreams were developed and managed through the 'Silver' response team, one of which is the 'Protect our People' plan to address new and emerging health and wellbeing risks posed by the pandemic.

The 'Protect our People' plan is data-driven and has been continuously reviewed and updated as the pandemic has gone on to ensure our colleagues have had access to the right support, at the right time, and that the business remained up to date on the health and wellbeing status of our colleagues and therefore able to make informed decisions around requirements for policy, standard and process updates, investment in tools and resources and other business resilience factors.

The remainder of this case study outlines all aspects covered within the 'Protect our People' plan.

Updating policies, standards and processes to reflect the new ways of working

As the way we work has evolved, whether that be working from home or on projects, we have had to adapt and evolve our existing policies, standards and processes – or produce Covid-specific addendums – to ensure we keep working in the safest, healthiest and most productive way.

We produced guidance for our line managers on supporting vulnerable colleagues and having good-quality wellbeing conversations with their team on navigating the complexities of the pandemic. We also introduced a number of policies including flexible working to support our parents and carers and an enhanced annual leave policy to encourage more frequent breaks.

Staying healthy while working from home

In the same way as working in the office, we wanted to ensure colleagues had access to equipment that would ensure their health is unharmed – a core concern being that they would be restricted to crouching over a small laptop for months. We therefore delivered monitors, keyboards, chairs, etc to the homes of anyone who requested them and fast-tracked specialist ergonomic equipment to those with medical need to ensure existing conditions were not exacerbated by working from home. In addition, we encouraged exercise and regular breaks from computers.

We also provided guidance on how to make the most of the home set-up to get the best possible ergonomic arrangement with limited equipment in comparison to the office. We provided guidance and a checklist on how employees could set themselves up, ensure they were working safely from home and seek support if they experienced any pain or discomfort during this time. Since then, we have relaunched our new 'remote working' display screen equipment (DSE) assessment to support employees who work from home, office and/or are roaming.

Communications, connection and digital enhancements

Throughout, we have ensured there are regular communications from the Mace executive board and senior leaders, keeping everyone aware of the circumstances and ensuring everyone remains connected – particularly important for those placed on furlough. The marketing and communications teams worked tirelessly to connect the business by delivering a full virtual events calendar, from breakfasts with the board to diversity and inclusion events, health and wellbeing events, business updates and knowledge- and success-sharing events.

A number of new employee-driven networks were developed from the ground up to support colleagues across the business. Women at Mace and Parents at Mace joined our existing Pride, Enabled,

FIGURE 9.1   Sample resource taken from digital campaign

WELLBEING MATTERS

TOP TIPS TO AVOID FATIGUE AND BOOST YOUR WELLBEING

Make sure you're taking breaks throughout the day. Change your meetings from 30 minutes and 1 hour, to 25 minutes and 50 minutes to give you and others a comfort break. For those on Windows 10, you can set these timings as your new default. Click here

New Meeting   25 MINS ✓ Accept   50 MINS ✓ Accept

Help to relieve the pressure to respond to emails out of core working hours by using the footer below in your email signature:

Name
Job title
Mace address
d xxxxxx m xxxxxxxxx
www.macegroup.com

At Mace we work flexibly, so if you receive this email at a time of day that is outside of your regular working pattern please do not feel that you need to respond or take any action outside of your own working hours.

Record your time accurately in Oracle Time Cards, including all extra hours worked. This data will help line managers and senior leaders to better support their teams.

Reduce the noise in your inbox and catch up with colleagues over the phone, rather than sending emails.

(continued)

Military and Wellbeing networks and were quickly introduced to raise awareness of the challenges these groups were experiencing and continue to drive the inclusion and wellbeing agendas across the business.

The networks, all made up of volunteers across the business going over and above their day jobs, and all supported and sponsored by members of Mace's senior leadership and executive board, gave colleagues a platform to seek support from their peers and take comfort that their experiences weren't isolated ones, to raise awareness of challenges faced, and share ideas and tips on how to manage and maintain their wellbeing.

FIGURE 9.1 (Continued)

In our new digital world, there are a number of individual actions we can all take to boost our wellbeing and reduce the risk of fatigue. Here are some simple techniques:

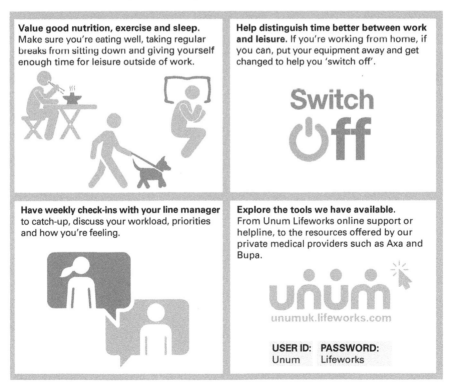

Our IT teams delivered the full Microsoft Teams package in a matter of weeks as opposed to the planned months to provide the business with better tools to work remotely and stay connected. Teaming up with the HR and Health, Safety and Wellbeing teams they introduced Microsoft Insights and Cortana to provide colleagues with the opportunity to reclaim balance and control in the virtual world by getting regular insights into their working habits, and plan in opportunities for breaks, focus time, personal time etc, which were at risk of getting lost as the boundaries between work and home life became increasingly blurred. The technology also provides individuals with the opportunity to track their mood throughout the week and identify patterns to make improvements using the platform. A campaign on avoiding fatigue and boosting wellbeing was used to deliver these new tools.

We encouraged line managers and colleagues to maintain regular contact with one another via phone and Microsoft Teams. We also suggested minimizing consumption of news, setting up a WhatsApp group or Teams chat with people in their team and speaking with their line manager regularly.

Our popular Conversations for Wellbeing training programme for line managers was quickly redeveloped into a virtual course to provide line managers with the confidence to have conversations around mental health, physical health and wellbeing in a virtual context as well as in a regular face-to-face environment. This programme is something we monitor regularly; previous research has told us that those in our business whose line managers talk to them often and always about their wellbeing are four times more likely to reveal a mental health condition at work – it was more important than ever that we continued to create a psychologically safe environment where colleagues who were struggling felt they could come forward. This also coincided with a new 'managing remotely' programme of workshops for line managers and a line manager hub full of resources to enable and empower line managers to build successful engaged teams remotely.

Data and information

We created a new Covid-19 section on our intranet home page and in the health, safety and wellbeing management system so that Covid-19-related processes, guidance and information were easy to find and access. Here we provided information and resources on all things related to maintaining health and wellbeing throughout the pandemic, with a particular focus on mental health. We understood that the extraordinary circumstances and evolving situation would be unsettling and worrying for many; those who continued to work on our projects could be concerned about the risk of exposure to themselves and loved ones, and equally those working at home for long periods of time could feel isolated, not to mention those furloughed or within the extremely clinically vulnerable category.

To ensure our business areas understood the unique challenges their teams were facing, we developed a 'how are you?' survey template and guidelines to enable them to issue their own mini surveys, enabling them to check in on colleagues and address any local issues quickly, as opposed to letting them build up and cause longer-term issues.

To continuously inform our Protect our People plan we also ran a regular Group-wide pulse survey to monitor the health and wellbeing status of our colleagues. We reviewed this data alongside other data sources such as the ongoing utilization of our employee assistance programmes (EAPs), our absence data, holiday uptake and our time-card data where colleagues log their hours worked to monitor any risk of fatigue or burnout across the business. We reviewed our own data against external data sources such as Mind's workforce surveys and the Morneau Shepell global mental health index to understand the impact on mental health and wellbeing that the pandemic was having in a broader context.

Knowing that the impact of the pandemic on mental health and wellbeing could be long lasting, we enhanced our data reporting processes for our annual engagement and wellbeing survey with

Robertson Cooper that was completed early 2021 to give the business more information than ever before on what drives health and wellbeing for Mace colleagues. Moving away from PDF reports, we built an online dashboard structured around our business hierarchy that breaks down the different areas of wellbeing across all levels of the organization. The dashboard allows business areas to self-serve, look across different demographics, and cut the data up into reports that suit their need.

Keeping people well with positive psychology

Being all too aware of the risks to our colleagues' mental health and wellbeing throughout the pandemic, the health and wellbeing team adapted the existing wellbeing calendar and began to introduce the concept of positive psychology to the business with a view to focus solely on the things that maintain and boost wellbeing and provide opportunities for colleagues to engage with and develop those areas that optimize wellbeing and prevent ill-health.

We adapted our existing campaign on the 'five ways to wellbeing' to incorporate virtual working and provide tips and tools on the five areas: be active, stay connected, give, keep learning and take notice. This included webinars, podcasts and information resource packs.

Throughout the year we continued to acknowledge national awareness days, particularly around mental health, and adapted our virtual events into forums to give colleagues the opportunity to discuss how they were feeling in a safe space. These events were extremely well attended and often peer-led to give as many people as possible an opportunity to share openly. We have since set up an events protocol for event organizers and the communications team to ensure that anyone who speaks out on our sessions has a follow-up and is well supported, and that the teams running the events have support in place and opportunities to debrief following particularly emotive sessions.

FIGURE 9.2 A screenshot of Mace's enhanced Engagement and Wellbeing dashboard

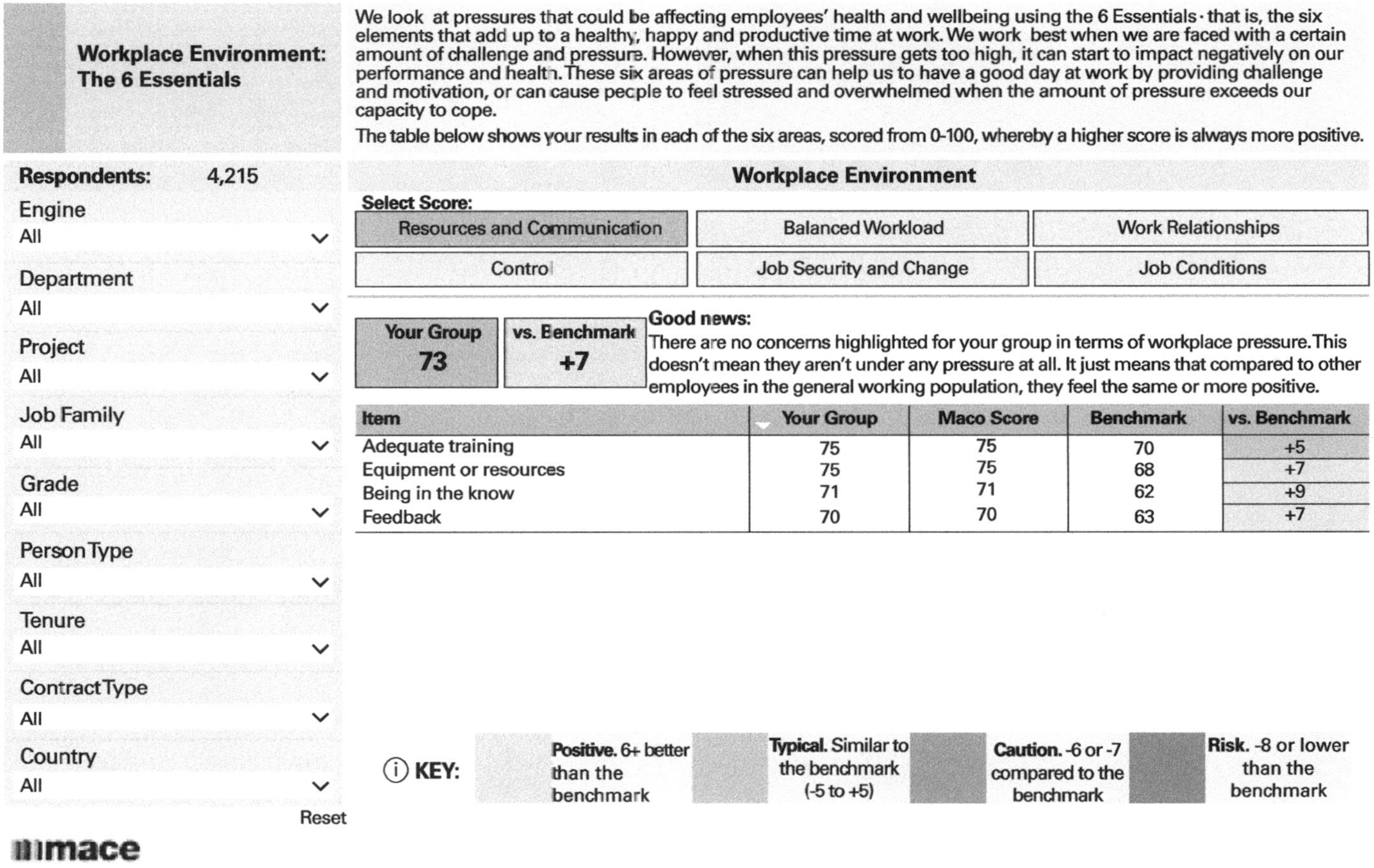

Workplace Environment: The 6 Essentials

We look at pressures that could be affecting employees' health and wellbeing using the 6 Essentials – that is, the six elements that add up to a healthy, happy and productive time at work. We work best when we are faced with a certain amount of challenge and pressure. However, when this pressure gets too high, it can start to impact negatively on our performance and health. These six areas of pressure can help us to have a good day at work by providing challenge and motivation, or can cause people to feel stressed and overwhelmed when the amount of pressure exceeds our capacity to cope.

The table below shows your results in each of the six areas, scored from 0-100, whereby a higher score is always more positive.

Workplace Environment

Select Score:

Resources and Communication	Balanced Workload	Work Relationships
Control	Job Security and Change	Job Conditions

Your Group	vs. Benchmark
73	+7

Good news:
There are no concerns highlighted for your group in terms of workplace pressure. This doesn't mean they aren't under any pressure at all. It just means that compared to other employees in the general working population, they feel the same or more positive.

Item	Your Group	Maco Score	Benchmark	vs. Benchmark
Adequate training	75	75	70	+5
Equipment or resources	75	75	68	+7
Being in the know	71	71	62	+9
Feedback	70	70	63	+7

Respondents: 4,215

Engine
All 〉

Department
All 〉

Project
All 〉

Job Family
All 〉

Grade
All 〉

Person Type
All 〉

Tenure
All 〉

Contract Type
All 〉

Country
All 〉

Reset

ⓘ **KEY:**

| Positive. 6+ better than the benchmark | Typical. Similar to the benchmark (-5 to +5) | Caution. -6 or -7 compared to the benchmark | Risk. -8 or lower than the benchmark |

⫴mace

FIGURE 9.3   Our calendar of wellbeing activities during the first lockdown period

WELLBEING ACTIVITIES

STAYING WELL IN CHALLENGING
TIMES – EMMA WRATH
13:30–14:30 28 APRIL

REGISTER HERE

PREVENTING AND REDUCING MUSCLE,
BONE AND JOINT PROBLEMS – BUPA

WATCH HERE

MADE TO MOVE: BECOME A
MOVEMENT OPPORTUNIST
16:00–16:40 7 MAY

REGISTER HERE

THE WINNING TEAM: FOSTER
PSYCHOLOGICAL SAFETY
16:00–16:40 14 MAY

REGISTER HERE

MAKING THE MOST OF WORKING
FROM HOME – BUPA

WATCH HERE

HOW TO HAVE CONVERSATIONS
ABOUT HEALTH – REMOTELY
11:30–13:00 5 MAY

REGISTER HERE

INFORMATION: VOLUNTEERING
DURING THE CORONAVIRUS
PANDEMIC

INFORMATION HERE

(continued)

FIGURE 9.3 (Continued)

LINE MANAGERS: HEALTHY
WORKING FROM HOME
11:30–12:30 1 MAY

REGISTER HERE

IMPROVING YOUR SLEEP – BUPA

WATCH HERE

SLEEP: YOUR WAKE UP CALL
16:00–16:40 21 MAY

REGISTER HERE

THRIVING CULTURE: ADOPTING
AN ABUNDANCE MINDSET
16:00–16:40 27 APRIL

REGISTER HERE

PODCAST: BUILDING RESILIENCE
PASSWORD: RES

WATCH HERE

FIND YOUR WORK-LIFE BALANCE –
BUPA

WATCH HERE

MANAGING STRESS – BUPA

WATCH HERE

EMOTIONAL AGILITY: TURNING
EMOTIONS INTO SUPERPOWERS
16:00–16:40 28 MAY

REGISTER HERE

PODCAST: DEALING WITH
CHANGE IN A POSITIVE WAY
PASSWORD: DWC

WATCH HERE

COMING SOON
Bupa will soon be releasing additional wellbeing videos about: self help,
mindfulness, keeping active at home, preventing and managing repetitive
strain injury (RSI).

COMING SOON HERE

Throughout all our communications and campaigns, the Health and Wellbeing team joined forces with Mace's HR team to ensure that at every opportunity Mace's health benefits were promoted and made visible – we knew the strain on the NHS and equivalent health authorities globally would impact access to medical advice and treatment for our colleagues, and wanted to ensure that everyone was aware of, and could access, the additional support that was available through Mace.

Our World Mental Health Day event 'Do One Thing' was one of our most well-attended events and focused on actions to maintain good mental health and boost resilience. Colleagues across the business shared their 'one thing' in advance of the event by filling in a postcard and sharing images across our social media platform to raise awareness.

Throughout the second half of 2020 we ran a three-month-long campaign called 'Getting personal with… positive psychology' with a focus on improving happiness, building on individual strengths and the things that keep us well. The proactive campaign wasn't to 'make light' of the very real risks to mental health and wellbeing at the time; we acknowledged that everyone had been impacted in one way or another, but we also wanted to do more by looking at mental health

FIGURE 9.4   Some of our Mace colleagues and their contribution to the 'do one thing' campaign

through a different, more positive and proactive lens, so that we were better equipped to tackle negative mental health before it became an issue. The campaign was focused on maximizing opportunities for increased wellbeing and resilience, covering subjects including resilience, focus, optimism, energy, connection and pressure – all areas of focus that when done well maintain good wellbeing.

Each topic had its own mini campaign and events series, resources for our wellbeing ambassadors, and tips/tools for colleagues and line managers with opportunities for individuals to engage by sharing their tips for maintaining/improving the areas of focus covered within the campaign.

Our global network of wellbeing ambassadors was integral to keeping the health wellbeing agenda at the forefront of colleagues' minds and was instrumental to the success of our calendar, driving all communications, resources etc locally and feeding back on challenges and need. As a result we have developed a full programme of engagement, recognition and CPD to ensure that our ambassadors and volunteer training instructors feel valued and supported for the hard work they put in to support their colleagues.

FIGURE 9.5 'Getting Personal with...' wrap up visual

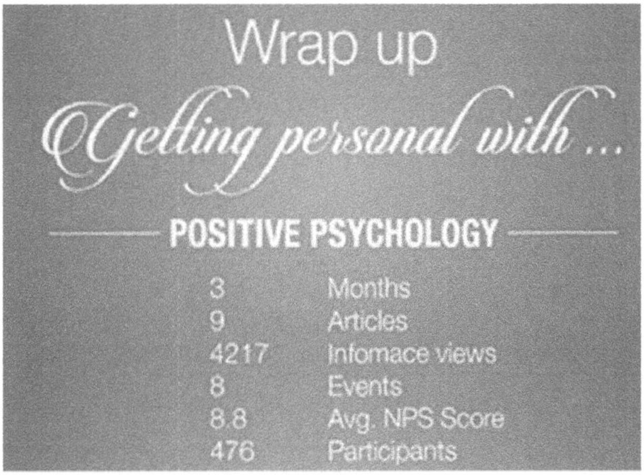

Covid-19 case response

Alongside the introduction of guidance, project and office operating procedures, and a vast number of resources available to guide the business in Covid-19 management, an internal support team was formed and given specific training on Covid-19, government guidance, Mace's internal Covid case and isolation reporting processes, and internal and external support available to people.

The purpose of the team was to respond to notifications of positive cases across the global business in Mace-run offices and projects by carrying out a detailed risk assessment, providing advice to Mace colleagues and supply chain on process, working with local health authorities and signposting people to support. We recognized that those impacted directly or indirectly by Covid-19 cases may experience difficult feelings and the team were there to act as a compassionate advisory service to ensure that those impacted were fully supported and knew where to access support in isolation. Aggregated and anonymous data was reported through the Covid-19 response team into data dashboards to demonstrate the volume of positive cases and Mace employee isolations, which enabled us to manage and monitor colleague health and team resilience to ensure disruptions to business activity were at a minimum.

Next steps

We recognize as a business that Covid-19 is far from over; the physical and psychosocial risks are here to stay, with more to uncover and manage as research around long Covid and other health outcomes matures over time.

With that in mind, the health and wellbeing team, in collaboration with key stakeholders, are in the process of developing a new strategic wellbeing plan that will redefine our approach to health and wellbeing at Mace. The plan will contribute to the successful delivery of both the business strategy and the health, safety and wellbeing strategy to 2026. It will be underpinned by intelligent data and informed by Mace colleagues from across the business and supply chain to create more good days at work for all – watch this space.

10

The CIPD'S pandemic response – supporting our organization and the people practitioners and communities we serve

PETER CHEESE

JENNY GOWANS

BRAD TAYLOR

The CIPD is the professional body for HR and people development, and our members have been at the very heart of the organizational response to the pandemic everywhere; they have rarely if ever worked harder. So in turn it has been a challenging year for us as an organization, supporting our members and the wider people profession and business community, but also responding to support our own people in these extraordinary circumstances.

As a result of the Covid-19 pandemic, this past year has been an enforced time of little social activity for us all. Our personal lives and social interactions have been restricted to the smallest of circles.

The impact on our working lives has been just as great, but far more varied. Frontline workers and sectors with heightened demand have struggled to deliver at scale while others have been forced to adapt to new ways of working, new business models, lack of demand and job losses. But what is certain is that all businesses, their leaders and their people have had to navigate and respond to a crisis the likes of which we have never seen before.

However, as with any crisis, there is also opportunity for positive change, and to take forward many lessons to improve the world of work and people's working lives.

To get to this point, where we can consider what lessons we carry forward from the pandemic, has been a tough journey that at times has felt relentless. CIPD research shows that many people are fatigued, that mental health through isolation has suffered, and that there are many concerns about the future. But many business leaders expect to make lasting and positive changes to the way the people in their organizations work. And in turn their people expect it.

Responding to the initial lockdowns

In February 2020, despite the emerging pandemic being all-consuming on every media channel, it was hard to believe that we were on the cusp of something that would so significantly impact all of our lives. But government response was ramping up quickly in all countries and in turn leadership teams were getting their organizations ready to navigate the challenges ahead. These teams, always including and often spearheaded by HR, were making decisions at pace.

Timing and restrictions enforced by governments varied around the world so for organizations with international operations the complexity increased. And one of the first lessons of the pandemic was learnt – leaders needed to trust their people and let operational decisions be made on the ground to keep pace with the changing local situation. We adopted this approach with our offices outside the UK; they knew what was best for their people, but at the same time we increased our touchpoints with them to ensure they still felt the support of the wider organization.

In the early phases of the pandemic, information and government guidance varied from being either very limited or overwhelming in its detail. At a time of uncertainty and heightened anxiety, trusted practical guidance and advice was urgently needed. We knew we had to step up as an organization to engage with our community, act as a channel to share experiences and provide guidance to a profession that was under a great deal of pressure.

By the end of March we had launched a dedicated coronavirus hub on our website to gather and share practical support and guidance, to disseminate and interpret official advice for members and non-members alike as we wanted our support to be accessible to all. The hub saw more than 2.2 million unique users, over 4 million page views, and 158,000 downloads in the first four months and continues to be a source of support through webinars, factsheets and guides updated daily to millions.

We spoke with our members, monitored social and community platform discussions and held daily meetings to discuss the most pressing needs of the profession, and to plan our response, not only for the profession but also to make recommendations to government.

Internally, we also had to work hard to adapt. We rapidly trialled new ways of remote working across multiple teams in the few days we had before leaving our offices prior to lockdown. Technology support was critical and we were fortunate in having recently implemented tools like Microsoft Teams, but the sudden shift to the whole organization working from home was a huge challenge. Like so many others, we were predominantly an office-based, desk-based, meeting room type of organization. One year later, and our people are adept at using collaborative technology; working together to achieve outcomes using video calls, instant messaging and working on shared documents and files.

From the outset, we knew we had to put our people first, focus on their needs and support, and to significantly increase our communications to help people feel connected and reassured in a time of great uncertainty.

Adapting our support to our members and other stakeholders

Within weeks, most employees and workers had fallen into one of three camps: those essential workers working from their usual places of work on the frontline, those able to work from home operating in a virtual world, and those where work was drying up and were already worrying about their futures.

Business leaders had to focus on keeping their businesses and workforces viable in rapidly changing circumstances and because of the lockdowns, in an economy that was being upended. Reassessing business models, financial forecasting and scenario planning became critical and frequent. It was clear that sustaining jobs was going to be a challenge. Rapid innovation was going to be needed.

At the CIPD we called on employers to put the wellbeing and financial security of their people first, and on policymakers to support businesses to do the right thing. We were quick to call for a UK Job Retention Scheme and among the first to suggest it be made as flexible as possible.

We consulted widely with legal experts and HR practitioners and published workforce planning guides to support organizations in planning how to manage their workforce in the light of reduced operations, and the new Job Retention Scheme and financial grants. We commissioned research into business response to the pandemic, and published a report on how trust and responsible leadership were key for survival.

Throughout, we recognized the need to gather vital evidence about the impact on jobs and working lives, so we surveyed the UK's employers and employees on a regular basis. To help inform public policy, we shared our insights directly with government departments, as well as issuing press statements to help influence employer practice and inform the public. Between March and June, we issued 19 press statements and featured in major news outlets across TV, radio and print media.

Adapting our own operating model and support to our people

And we applied all of this to ourselves as an organization. We balanced workloads where possible and prioritized looking after our workforce. We assessed our business model, revised our budgets and forecasts, and innovated our products and services.

As lockdowns stopped all face-to-face conferences, events and training, all of which had been central to our business model, we had to adapt. In eight weeks we moved the Festival of Work, our annual conference and exhibition, from a two-day live event to a virtual platform and allowed members to attend free of charge. Over 26,000 people registered to attend the event that was providing vital support and guidance to our members. We learnt that we could do this, and in short time.

We switched as much face-to-face training as possible to online, digitized more of our content, and created a number of new learning programmes in response to changing demand. And we recognized that many of our members would be in more difficult financial circumstances. In response, we froze our membership fees and provided some support for those who were struggling to pay.

With all these actions, not only did we sustain our membership numbers but we also saw growth and significant improvements in member satisfaction.

Our leaders at every level stepped up, greatly increasing our internal communications and looking after our people. As CEO I was doing weekly video updates and regular briefings to help everyone understand how we were responding, and what we saw as important. But also acknowledging that we didn't have all the answers and would have to adapt as we went along – reality and a degree of humility, but also trying to instil confidence that by working together we would get through these times, and could even thrive as a result.

Keeping in touch with our people also meant regularly surveying them on how they were feeling. We used our existing voice and communication channels, but also surveys directly asking about people's working environments and support needs. As our research has shown, many organizations have been able to do as we did and have maintained or even increased productivity and engagement.

Continuously adapting as more challenges emerge

The pandemic wasn't the only thing happening over the year of 2020 that businesses had to adapt to. As the UK formally ceased to be a member of the EU at the end of January 2020, the timing could hardly have been worse. The UK was also having to establish new trading relationships in a post-Brexit world, migration patterns started to shift, new regulations needed to be developed, and businesses were looking for clarity.

For us, as for so many, a further significant challenge and wake-up call came with the death of George Floyd in Minneapolis. We felt for the anger and frustration of our black and ethnic minority colleagues who were already dealing with the pressures of the pandemic. And we felt the pressure of needing to help our members and organizations support their people too.

Our policy and research teams that needed to work on this were already tired from their efforts on our coronavirus work. But inclusion is core to our purpose, so we rallied and reaffirmed our commitment to our own inclusion and diversity action plan and used our learnings from our coronavirus response to launch a hub and campaign to support organizations to end racism at work.

Throughout this period, organizations were dealing with people who were increasingly emotionally and mentally exhausted. The stresses from new ways of working, uncertainty, as well as the issues people were dealing with in their personal lives outside of work were taking their toll.

Our support for businesses needed to reflect this so we produced additional guidance to help support workforces in areas such as sickness, bereavement, screen fatigue, virtual onboarding, home schooling and caring and shielding, which we knew would support wellbeing.

It was clear also that as the pandemic progressed and with the additional challenges that came, business leaders and people professionals were also exhausted. We needed to support their wellbeing too, and celebrate their commitment and success, so we launched a member wellbeing helpline and a campaign called #HRtogether, stories from the People Profession. Our worldwide community of HR, L&D and other people professionals shared stories of how organizations from different sectors and industries have responded and adapted to the Covid-19 crisis and put people first. Recognition in times like this is critically important.

Learning from the pandemic

The last year has shown us all that work can be different and that organizations can operate in different ways. There is an expectation that we should all learn from this time and improve work, working patterns and cultures for the better.

Our traditional patterns of work, the standard working week and working hours, have been with us for generations, including a bias towards presenteeism and prevalence of command-and-control cultures.

A big stimulus has been needed to change beliefs and perceptions, to move us on from rule-based cultures and trust our people more, and to focus on outputs, not just hours worked.

We can implement change faster than we expected and many organizations, including ours, have proven this with adapting business models and technology uptake.

Leadership also has changed. Not only in how leaders communicate and connect, being more open and transparent, and a sense of less hierarchy, but also in how leaders navigate and deal with uncertainty.

We have also had to reconsider how we define the workplace. For many organizations, a place of work is wherever work can be achieved effectively utilizing modern communication and collaboration techniques and technology. Remote, home and hybrid working are all possible alternatives. There will be many practical and logistical issues to be worked through, but this is a huge opportunity to shift longstanding patterns of work and work paradigms.

Research consistently shows that most people would prefer a mix of time at home and at the office. Having more choice and flexibility can greatly contribute to managing and reducing stress and allow better integration of home and work commitments. It can therefore also support greater inclusion, giving more access to more people to have productive and fulfilling jobs and work opportunities.

But the pandemic has also reminded us of the importance of social contact and connection. Finding the right balance will take time – many people themselves will take time to adapt to new ways of working, including how we all manage our time, deal with the blurring of work-life boundaries and different types of stress that can come from home working. This is why choice and balance of where and how people work will be so important.

We will also need to work a lot harder to train line managers and people managers everywhere to understand and support more diverse teams with more diverse ways of working. We have to ensure that we create cohesive, collaborative workplaces that do not advantage people who work one way over another and that keep fairness and equity at the heart of their thinking so that we don't end up with two-tier or disparate systems.

All of this also has implications for how we hire people, on both a permanent and temporary basis. Collaborative technologies can be used to spread resources across regions, nations and borders. It can provide us with real flexibility in our workforces, enabling organizations to more readily scale up and down and dial in new talent from much more diverse locations.

Looking ahead – what needs to change

While the pandemic affected us all, certain groups of society suffered more. We were all in the same storm, but we were in different boats.

The burden of home schooling and childcare often fell to women, who were also more likely to suffer job losses. Evidence is also showing that older and younger workers were more likely to lose their jobs. At the sharper end, risk of death from Covid-19 was higher among black and minority ethnic people.

We must find a way to come together as societies, workforces and as a people. Every person should be able to fulfil their potential at work and to see work as a safe place to be themselves. Employers who take action to support equal progression and participation in the workplace, and who recognize the individual needs of their people, will grow their talent pool and build lasting engagement with their employees.

Now more than ever, there must be a strong focus on wellbeing at the heart of building responsible, sustainable businesses for the future. Furthermore, it's usually a question of choices rather than resources. We must engrain 'people first thinking' into our working practices and people management. Physical and mental wellbeing must be a priority, and giving people more choice for how, where and when they work will be a positive enabler.

Enabling all of this will help to make people more engaged and productive in their work, while giving businesses agility in their operations.

The pandemic has also brought into sharp relief the question of what we value as a society. Eyebrows have been raised over excessive executive pay in recent years and it became clear early in the pandemic that it was people on the frontline, often in lower-paid jobs, who were our most essential workers. Hospital staff, delivery drivers, retail workers, teachers, bus drivers, care home workers and more all played a huge role in keeping the wheels of our society turning. We honoured them with a weekly clap for key workers and had a low tolerance when we saw people being treated unfairly.

The gratitude of society to our key workers is clear, but it's unclear how these roles will be valued and rewarded by organizations in the 'new normal'. Fairness will be a key theme for organizations, covering pay and reward but also access to opportunity, development and progression and flexible working opportunities regardless of role.

Inequalities will limit not just the potential of individuals but our organizations as well.

Throughout the pandemic there's been a high expectation that organizations should do the right thing, and that they have a clear responsibility and duty of care to their workers and their community, not just their shareholders.

People professionals should be a driving force behind responsible business and corporate governance practices in organizations. This will ensure that key people-related issues – such as culture, reward equity, inclusion and employee voice – get the right attention at board level and are part of the executive team's decision-making process.

However, businesses all operate in a social context. And social change is demanding greater transparency, more responsible and ethical business, more fairness and inclusion, and demonstrable action by leaders to show they are listening and responding to what is going on in the world around them. These act as big drivers in engaging with employees, retaining and attracting talent, as well as reputation and brand image.

The pandemic has been a big catalyst and we can't let that pass. People don't stop being people when they come to work. And if businesses and leaders care for the things their people care about, they will care for the things the business cares about.

11

Reflections on the coronavirus pandemic at Rolls-Royce – one year in

DAVID ROOMES

Corporate Medical Directors, and other business risk managers around the world, have long known about the threat of a global pandemic. It has always been recognized by these professionals as a case of 'when', not 'if'. The challenge of course is that the nature and timing of any such threat is extremely difficult to predict and as such, proactive mitigation becomes difficult. Strategically, businesses do look at megatrends and take a longer-term view but operationally, they run to the cadence of the financial year. Targets, objectives, budgets and incentives are set annually, and allocating resources to a threat that may happen in one year's time or 30 inevitably and understandably results in the risk being de-prioritized by decision-makers. In conjunction with the unpredictability of the timing of the threat, the risk has been further deprioritized by resource allocators because of their perception of how other infectious disease threats have played out in recent years. Since the turn of the century, the world has been confronted with numerous infectious disease outbreaks such as SARS (2003), H1N1 (2009), MERS (2012), Zika (2015) and Ebola (2013–16). While these were all very significant epidemics and pandemics that made headlines at the time, the eventual outcome was that they were managed and contained and the overall impact on society and business was relatively minimal. It's not surprising therefore that wider society, including businesses, had become complacent about the threat. The implicit assumption was that highly disruptive global pandemics were a feature of times gone by and that the technological advances of the 21st century had relegated such events to the history books.

With an approximately 50 per cent market share of the large aero engine market, Rolls-Royce derives a significant proportion of its revenue from long-haul air travel. This business model is therefore adversely affected by events that disrupt air travel. The terrorist attacks of 9/11, the 2008 Global Financial Crisis and the 2011 volcanic ash cloud from the Icelandic mountain Eyjafjallajökull, are examples of events that significantly impacted global aviation and associated business sectors. Given the exposure to this type of threat, a global pandemic event had long been on the Group risk register and in recent years, the likelihood rating had been increased. Scenario and business continuity planning were undertaken periodically based on certain assumptions. Most pandemic planners worked on a broad hypothesis that a global pandemic event would take the form of a zoonosis and originate in the Far East, given the existence of 'wet markets' and the close interaction between humans and animals. Despite recent experience of SARS and MERS, both of which are due to coronaviruses, most planning has historically been based on influenza virus models.

The first reports from Wuhan in January 2020 were quickly shared among the various corporate medical director networks and, as matters escalated, widely reported in the media. As it became apparent that this was not an outbreak that would be contained locally or in-region, the company incident management framework was activated in order to ensure a timely and appropriate response to events as they unfolded. The Incident Support Team (IST) was stood up and as a starting point identified two overriding objectives: firstly to protect the health, safety and wellbeing of all our people, and secondly to limit business disruption with a focus on factories and operations. The remainder of this case study will focus on people aspects.

The health and wellbeing impacts of the pandemic have been profound, and the full scale of these impacts is not yet fully understood. Clearly there are the impacts of the disease itself on those unfortunate enough to contract it. The physical effects range across a spectrum from the minor to the catastrophic and the severity of such symptoms depends on myriad factors such as age, ethnicity and the presence of co-morbidities. The immediate imperative at the outset of the pandemic was therefore to reduce the risk of viral transmission to as low as reasonably possible. Following government guidance and a range of other sources, steps were implemented to create 'Covid-secure' workplaces. Anyone who could work safely and effectively from home was required to do so and to continue to do so in line with local regulations and guidance prevailing in their location. Those who were deemed to be essential workers were permitted to be in the workplace but were required to follow strict risk-mitigation measures with a strong emphasis on behavioural controls primarily based on strict hygiene and distancing measures.

Having implemented 'Covid-secure' controls, the second priority was to consider how best to support the wellbeing of our people. Given the very significant adverse impact on the aviation sector, the impacts felt in broader society were to some extent magnified for the Rolls-Royce workforce. In order to secure the future of the business (and thereby employment for the majority of employees and future generations), it was quickly apparent that an urgent business restructuring programme would need to be implemented. The announcement of a reduction in the size of the global workforce of greater than 15 per cent inevitably led to high levels of uncertainty, insecurity and anxiety. Alongside the need to support those colleagues whose roles were at risk, was the need to support colleagues who suddenly found themselves working from home for an extended and indefinite time. Uncertainty, insecurity, isolation, and for some people, loss and bereavement, have been ever-present risks to psychological wellbeing throughout the pandemic. Additional pressures have come in the form of home-schooling for some and concerns over the wellbeing of elderly and vulnerable loved ones for many. The strain on personal relationships has been highlighted by published statistics regarding increases in domestic violence and a key part of any business response had to be that any vulnerable employee has access to the security of the workplace should they need it. Any such arrangement needed to be managed sensitively and confidentially, typically with the involvement of HR and Occupational Health.

The pandemic response in terms of supporting the health and wellbeing of people required close collaboration between multiple stakeholders, all of whom had an important part to play. Subject matter expertise was led by the Occupational Health and Wellbeing team supported by HSE, HR, IT, Security, Property, Facilities and others. In addition, the importance of partnering with internal communications cannot be overstated. From the outset of the crisis in January 2020, it was clear that the company needed to provide clear, credible and consistent advice to employees, all of whom were anxious to understand how the organization was responding and what would be expected of them as the situation developed.

A 'Covid microsite' was set up on the intranet homepage with the understanding that this would become the 'single source of truth' and a one-stop shop for all resources relating to the pandemic. A framework was established recognizing the different roles and needs of different types of workers, and resources developed or adapted to help them manage their own physical and mental wellbeing and, if applicable, that of their team. IT were quick to ramp up bandwidth to enable secure remote logon as thousands of workers suddenly found themselves simultaneously working from home. An accelerated implementation programme was also initiated to move to the Microsoft Teams platform to enable more effective collaboration. Removing IT frustrations and obstacles played an important part in improving employees' experience of home working and thus their perceived wellbeing.

In addition to regular communication and improved IT, a detailed review and, where necessary, revision of our mental health resources was undertaken. Our established approach is to develop knowledge, skills and confidence to empower and enable employees at all levels in the organization to look after their own mental health, recognize the needs of colleagues and to access support when required. Emphasis is placed on helping managers understand the particular challenges and risks created by remote working and a range of tools, resources and materials were curated and made available on the Covid microsite. Regular wellbeing check-ins are now encouraged as an integral part of team meetings and one-to-ones. Guidance is available on how to hold a boundaried conversation about mental wellbeing and where to signpost to for professional support when required. A global network of mental health champions has been expanded to support employees and their managers to access such support. For those with acute mental health needs, the Employee Assistance Programme (EAP) is globally available and other support is available through Occupational Health in some countries. There is recognition of the fact that psychological distress may be (and usually is) the result of a combination of work and non-work-related factors and therefore, advice on matters such as financial and legal issues is also available.

Moving suddenly to new ways of working necessitated a rapid review and adaptation of the HR policy framework. Understanding the potential impacts to terms and conditions as well as the legal and insurance implications was important to get right both for the peace of mind of employees and to ensure that the company was meeting its legal obligations. Many employees adapted quickly to remote working and found the advantages to have an overall positive impact on their sense of wellbeing. Not commuting and more time spent with family have been widely cited as upsides. However, these individual benefits may be offset by less strong relationships with one's team and an eroding of the psychological impact between the organization and employees. Onboarding new employees and integrating them into existing teams is particularly difficult to do remotely. Balancing these pros and cons in the post-pandemic hybrid workplace will be key.

Remote working has been particularly challenging for some individuals. Those with underlying health conditions that place them at significantly increased risk to the harms of Covid-19 have had to deal with increased levels of anxiety as well as greater isolation as they have shielded. Similarly, those workers who live alone have experienced a greater sense of social isolation and disconnect. Many families sharing limited living space for work and schooling have had to endure sub-optimal workstation set-ups and, in some cases, poor internet connectivity, which has added further to the burden.

We recognize the strong relationship between physical and mental wellbeing and our approach during the pandemic has addressed this. Resources were developed and deployed giving employees guidance on how to maintain healthy habits during lockdowns. Exercise, sleep and nutrition are components of wellbeing that are easily derailed by disruption to an individual's normal routines. Working from non-standard workstations has also increased the risk to musculoskeletal health and a comprehensive risk management process has been developed and implemented on a mandatory basis. Where necessary, equipment is provided in order to help optimize ergonomic set-ups.

In any crisis, the role of leadership becomes critical. Generally people find it reassuring to know that decision-makers have all the correct information, tools and resources to hand to enable them to make confident decisions that will ensure the survival of the business and to protect the health, safety and wellbeing of the people who work there. Enabling leaders and managers has been a core part of the approach taken during the pandemic. From a health and wellbeing perspective, this has been achieved by ensuring access to evidence-based information rooted in science to ensure that where advice or information is offered, it is authoritative and reliable. Having trusted internal medical resource is a definite advantage in a health crisis such as a global pandemic. Not only does this give business leaders access to an informed source on all technical aspects but importantly, the organization also gains access to a rich network of corporate medical directors covering multiple specialities and hundreds of years of collective corporate medical experience. What distinguishes these medical specialists is their ability to navigate between the academic, the clinical and the business worlds and to understand the realities and practical implications of different courses of action. A feature of the pandemic has been how quick entrepreneurs have been to try to capitalize on the crisis, with thousands of companies springing up overnight to offer 'Covid solutions' ranging from cleaning products and PPE to testing systems and tech-based 'Covid passports'. It is unquestionably desirable to have in-house expertise on hand if the organization is to avoid implementing costly, often ineffective and sometimes harmful, interventions.

Recognizing and considering the importance of individual health beliefs and cultural differences is essential for successful communication on all matters pertaining to health and wellbeing. This is equally true in a health crisis. Getting the tone of communications right requires the input of professional communications experts so that messages are trusted, believed and acted upon. Given how much of the Covid response relies on individuals complying with and adhering to behavioural controls, providing the rationale behind the message is key. Generally, if people understand why they are being asked to do something and it is not too difficult to do, one achieves greater levels of uptake and compliance. This has been borne out by the experience in the company and also in wider society. Working with trades unions and employee representatives was also important in ensuring that messaging reached all levels of the organization, especially the 'hard to reach', typically those without regular access to company IT.

In a crisis such as the current pandemic, corporate medical directors are often challenged by the question, 'what else should we be doing to support the health and wellbeing of our people?' The question is a legitimate one and we should always be exploring the art of the possible but at the same time, one has to be careful to manage expectations. It's unrealistic to expect people to feel good about a global pandemic, and loss of employment in particular can be devastating in an economic crisis with a shrinking job market. Very difficult decisions need to be taken by business leaders and it is important to recognize that they too are employees with fears, concerns and insecurities who may have psychological needs that require support. The most important elements of any response are clarity of communication and ensuring that employees are treated with dignity and respect.

At the time of writing, the pandemic is far from over and there are still many unknowns, both about the primary impacts of the disease itself but also about the secondary health and wellbeing impacts. 'Long Covid' is a condition that is only just starting to be described and the longer-term sequelae of this syndrome will only be understood in the fullness of time. Since it seems to afflict mainly those of working age, it is a condition that needs to be on the radar of all occupational health and HR professionals. Much has also been written about the anticipated mental health impacts of the pandemic. Again, time will provide more fulsome answers, but it is reasonable to expect that many people could experience a post-traumatic-type response to events. This is particularly true for those who have suffered job losses and/or unexpected bereavement. Thinking ahead to anticipate the needs of these groups should be part of planning for the post-pandemic workplace and workforce.

Finishing on a positive note, it is true that many individuals have described significant improvements in their overall subjective wellbeing status. Reduced commuting times, more time with family and increased opportunity for exercise have been real benefits for many. The challenge will be to sustain the positive health benefits for those fortunate enough to have experienced them and to mitigate the negative health impacts for those who haven't. One thing that has been made abundantly clear by the events of 2020–21 is that the wellbeing of society is founded on the health and wellbeing of individuals and it is incumbent on employers everywhere to do what they can to protect and enhance the health of their workers.

12

John Lewis Partnership

Managing wellbeing in a crisis

NICK DAVISON
This chapter sets out the approach taken by the John Lewis Partnership in managing the wellbeing of its Partners (staff) during the Covid-19 pandemic in 2020/21.

Context

The John Lewis Partnership owns and operates two of Britain's best-loved retail brands – John Lewis and Waitrose. Started as a radical idea nearly a century ago, the Partnership is the largest employee-owned business in the UK and among the largest in the world, with over 80,000 employees who are all Partners in the business. Profits made are reinvested into the business – for customers and Partners.

Partners work across shops, online, distribution and support functions through the head office, from a network of 470 locations within the UK, the Channel Islands, and our sourcing offices in Hong Kong and India. Waitrose is the only UK supermarket to operate its own farm, supplying our Waitrose shops with key products. Since 1953 we have also operated our own textile factory where we make John Lewis own-brand soft furnishings, duvets and pillows, all Made to Measure seven-day service curtains, and roman and roller blinds. We also own five Partnership hotels specifically for Partners and their families and friends to use at a specially subsidized rate. And we also have an installation team working within customers' homes.

The nature of Waitrose as a food retailer and John Lewis as a non-food retailer meant that the business could not operate consistently as one through the pandemic restrictions, with Waitrose trading throughout as an essential retailer and to help 'feed the nation', while John Lewis as a non-essential retailer was forced to close for extended periods before finally reopening in April 2021.

With John Lewis shops shut and the significant growth in supermarket grocery delivery, both brands experienced substantial online trading growth and supply chain pressure to fulfil these increased channel and delivery demands. Also, with head office Partners working from home, Partners had very different experiences depending on where they worked.

As an employee-owned business, looking after our Partners is key. We've been investing in Partners' health and wellbeing since 1929 – 19 years before the NHS – when we introduced free in-house health and medical services to all our Partners.

Today, this continues through our Partnership Health Services team, with over £20 million invested annually. Partnership Health Services is a multidisciplinary clinical team which includes occupational health nurses, a doctor, physiotherapist and wellbeing clinical lead. Within this, we have a unique Partner Support service, which provides Partners with emotional, practical and financial support. This confidential, non-judgemental listening phone service is run by specially trained Partners.

How the pandemic challenged organizational wellbeing

Trading conditions

In March 2020 the impact of Covid-19 on UK society became very clear. International travel restrictions came into force, the UK Government closed schools, introduced 'Stay at Home' instructions and closed non-essential shops and hospitality venues. There was an immediate reaction in supermarkets, with panic buying commonplace despite reassurances that there were sufficient stocks of food items. Waitrose Partners working on the shop floor experienced the extremes of customer behaviours as people panicked, sometimes over the least obvious items. Unsurprisingly, there was immediate pressure on Waitrose.com for a significant increase in online grocery and delivery orders. Typically, Waitrose had been delivering 60,000 orders per week to customers' homes at the beginning of the pandemic; this was scaled to 240,000 weekly deliveries.

In John Lewis shops Partners were sent home initially as their shops were shut, with In Home Services also suspended, but supply chain remained open throughout, servicing the growth in online sales and deliveries. The benefit of being one Partnership with two brands is that more than 4,500 Partners from John Lewis were redeployed to Waitrose during the various lockdowns, helping to keep the nation fed and help as absence levels rose.

The impact on Partners' wellbeing

With 80,000 Partners, individuals experienced a range of different impacts at different times through the pandemic. Initially, there was great uncertainty and shock, with people seeking more information and certainty, which drove significant increases in calls to our support services. Emotions ran high, especially for those with potentially higher risk profiles such as having underlying health conditions, or those trying to understand what implications it had for them. The loss of individual control in decision making was also seen as a factor; central government decisions designed to reduce the infection spread had an impact on where you could go and who (if anybody) you could meet, which was reinforced with typically negative media and social media coverage.

More tangibly, absence levels rose significantly as the infection rate increased, self-isolation was required, and shielding for the clinically vulnerable was introduced. This was a very dynamic picture, with significant regional variations, but at its peak, over 12,000 Partners were not available to work.

After the initial shock, as the extent of the pandemic and its effects became clearer, emotions became more negative, with fear and sadness common. The impacts of isolation, fear of catching the virus as the infection rate and death toll rose, or being vulnerable, all played their part.

Analysis of Partner phone calls into our Partner Support services highlighted that personal symptoms, vulnerability/shielding, self-isolation, living with somebody vulnerable, returning to work, care responsibilities and financial implications caused the greatest anxiety.

However, over time, as a 'new normal' was established, Partners working in their normal environments generally adjusted to the new ways that society and work operated, with a keen focus on remaining safe. However, it was also evident that the ongoing uncertainty impacting the whole of people's lives had raised sustained levels of anxiety across a broader spectrum, especially for those who were working from home or were furloughed.

Working parents became home-schoolers, home became a work environment even if it wasn't suitable to be one, and many people were unable to work through no fault of their own. This didn't actually translate into more requests for direct mental health support but was seen in increased registrations to use Unmind, our positive psychology app, to over 10,000 Partners. It was also evident in the worsening severity of the cases assessed and progressed for cognitive behaviour therapy treatment, suggesting that those with existing psychological challenges were hit particularly hard.

Insight from Partners' use of Unmind highlighted that the most prevalent feelings were tiredness, anxiety and frustration, with the most-used educational series being 'Navigating Covid-19' as Partners sought to understand more about the disease. The lowest Partner scores were for calmness, fulfilment and sleep, while a sense of connection remained the strongest. It was interesting to note that in March and April 2020 the index scores for these sentiments fell significantly, but reverted in May 2020 to pre-Covid levels where they consistently remained for the rest of the year, suggesting that these Partners were adjusting to the new environment.

How did we respond?

The Partnership was quick to implement crisis management plans, establishing a 'Silver Group' of cross-functional leaders, led by two members of the executive team. All Covid-19-related activity and communications were channelled through this group, providing a simple and decisive decision-making channel. The underlying principles of the Partnership's response were:

1 safety first, in relation to both customers and Partners;

2 adherence to government and public health authority guidance;

3 working from home wherever possible.

Key organizational actions were:

- Quick adoption and reinforcement of hand hygiene/face coverings/signage/social distancing/enhanced cleaning protocols/queue marshalling to create the safest possible shopping and working environment. This was recognized by customers and Partners alike.

- Communication – a single-channel Covid-19 communication hub established for the whole business, managed centrally and updated daily.

- Clinically vulnerable Partners were asked to stay at home to shield, in line with government guidance, and to complete 'Wellbeing Action Plans' with their managers, which have been maintained over time, to manage their specific personal risks.

- Introduction of centralized reporting of positive Covid-19 cases, self-isolation and absence tracking to assist resource planning.

- We became one of the first UK businesses to pilot and roll out workplace rapid lateral flow Covid-19 testing for our Partners across our shops and supply chain sites.

- We supported the NHS by repurposing space at our head office in Bracknell into a vaccination centre, provided hotel accommodation for medical staff in Hampshire, and donated care packages for frontline NHS workers.

Delivery of wellbeing services

The Partnership's Occupational Health Service and Partner Support teams were reorganized to provide a national virtual call centre, providing access to Partners across the business. In seven weeks across March–April 2020 the teams handled over 9,000 calls from Partners. Other adjustments to the support delivery model were made and these are set out below:

Psychological wellbeing

Telephone support continued to be provided for Partners to address Covid-19, mental health and life concerns and was delivered by Partnership Health Services and Partner Support six days per week, over extended operating hours. The team answered on average 4,000 calls per month from working Partners and 1,000 calls per month from retired Partners.

Partners requiring more formal support continued to be referred for virtual or telephone-based counselling or cognitive behaviour therapy and were case-managed remotely by the clinical team.

Based on the initial insight from Partners' concerns, short videos were launched, focused on Managing Isolation, Managing Relationships and Managing Bereavement, which all became evident factors during the pandemic.

There was a specific focus on Partner resilience, and a free 'Resilience Snapshot' was conducted in collaboration with Robertson Cooper, the business psychologists, with 6,250 Partners taking part; many received for the first time a personalized view of their own resilience. The aggregated results showed that Partners benchmarked well against pre-Covid resilience levels of other benchmarked organizations and showed strong levels of commitment and productivity compared to that comparator. The results also showed impacts on the symptoms of mental health and from the degree of change taking place.

These indicators encouraged a continued focus on developing Partners' self-awareness and self-determination, to equip them for these turbulent and uncertain times. Unmind launched a Building

Resilience – Growing Through Challenging Times educational series with a dedicated Partner workbook. We made four Silver Cloud self-managing modules (the psychological therapy tool) available to all Partners free of charge. These included Space for Resilience, Space for Sleep, Space from Stress, and Space from Covid-19. We also reinforced remote working guidance on our own Partner Development Website and internal intranet.

Physical wellbeing

Naturally, the greatest emphasis in relation to physical wellbeing focused on remaining safe and free from Covid-19, routinely following hygiene, social distancing and limiting personal contact. However, beyond that, physiotherapy continued to be provided to Partners but was delivered virtually, scaling the existing Physio Advice Line service provided by Physio Med to provide virtual consultations.

The Partnership Health Services team introduced a clinical evaluation tool, developed by the University of Southampton, to assist the triage process in the evaluation of individual risk factors in relation to Covid-19 and other underlying health conditions. This was actively used in assessing return to work consultations.

Virtual daily exercise classes were initially broadcast from the Waitrose Bracknell Sports Centre before being extended to include online yoga, pilates and strength classes. Neck, lower back and shoulder videos were published to encourage the maintenance of good posture and head office Partners were able to order office equipment such as desks, chairs and computer screens for their homes.

Diabetes screening was undertaken in London, where the Partnership has a high concentration of shops and Partners, between lockdowns to highlight the very different outcomes experienced by diabetics with Covid-19, especially in different ethnic communities.

In addition, a 12-week Eat Well, Feel Well campaign managed by our Waitrose Nutrition Manager and Wellbeing Clinical Lead was run to help Partners make positive lifestyle choices, especially in relation to their diet and exercise. This programme was re-run in 2021.

The cycle to work salary sacrifice scheme was extended and promoted to reinforce the importance of activity, especially during lockdown, along with promoting the Partnership's 24 clubs and societies.

Social wellbeing

The Partnership has an active membership of its internal Partner Choice leisure and social brand, with 45,000 active Partners engaging regularly. In 2019 the website had over 16 million hits and the attendance of Partners and their families at events, clubs, concerts, theme parks and the Partnership's five hotels ran into the tens of thousands.

Covid-19 had a direct impact in this area by restricting personal interaction and limiting social contact in unprecedented ways. However, rather than accept the limitations imposed by the lockdown, our social wellbeing programmes were converted, wherever possible, to a digital equivalent. The new content attracted 125,000 hits in its first month alone and included:

- A 'Keeping Connected' hub was launched – particularly focused on enabling those who were furloughed to stay connected.

- A weekly 'Feel Good Friday' programme was established, which brought a range of different content, including learning something new, bringing the outside in, fun stuff to do with the kids, and even a commemorative edition in May remembering the 75th anniversary of VE day.

- Through Partner Choice, a daily virtual challenge 'Knight School' was created to entertain and occupy younger children while the schools were closed, centred on our own Brownsea Castle. On a wider scale, Partner Choice maintained regular weekly engagement with 45,000 Partners throughout the pandemic period.

- A virtual Rock Choir was set up to rehearse and then perform a virtual rendition of Abba's Super Trouper.

- A series of Partner quizzes were hosted on Sunday evenings.

- Partner Choice TV was established, attracting nearly 1,000 subscribers. Experts within the business shared tips from their areas of expertise. Gardeners and landscapers from Odney and Leckford provided tips for gardeners, 'On the Farm' provided insight into the daily operations at the Partnership's Leckford Estate, and Partnership chefs provided cookery lessons.

- Partnership Radio was set up, providing a weekly Thursday morning radio show. It became very popular among head office and supply chain Partners and was a fantastic means of recognizing great achievements and giving individual callouts, with the ability to personalize the messages.

- Digital connection: the Partnership already used Google as its email software. Google Currents communities were already well established as a popular way of communicating and sharing across a wide variety of social, lifestyle, business, team and personal interest topics, and significantly across traditional business structures and formal communication channels. Partnership Pets remains the largest community – we all love our pets! During the pandemic the use of Google Currents became more significant as a means of staying in touch virtually with others.

- Historically, John Lewis Partnership has hosted bi-annual social events for its retired Partner population, in the Summer and at Christmas. The obvious risks to older members of society from Covid-19 and the lockdown restrictions meant that this wasn't possible in 2020. Instead, virtual Christmas events were arranged, including festive decoration and mince pie making, along with Christmas carols.

Social cohesion and a strong sense of Partnership team identity have always been important within the Partnership. The physical lockdown restrictions made maintaining those personal networks and contact difficult in many areas but the effort applied to providing virtual alternatives where possible maintained a sense of engagement and belonging for many Partners.

Financial wellbeing

The Partnership has historically provided financial assistance to Partners through a programme of loans and grants, based on financial need. These were maintained throughout the pandemic. Initially it was envisaged that demand for this support would increase. However, that has not materialized, in part due to the Partnership's decision to maintain 100 per cent salaries for those unable to work due to forced non-essential shop closures during the various lockdowns and shielding, and the reduction in many lifestyle costs due to lockdown. The start of the pandemic also coincided with the launch of a three-year financial education programme, 'Money Smart', designed to improve financial understanding and planning capabilities. This work is ongoing.

What about the future?

The Partnership has used these extraordinary times to also look to the future of the organization, seeking to redefine its purpose, values and strategic direction, reflecting the very real changes in the retail industry that have been accelerated by Covid-19. As these are brought to life over the next five years through our Partnership Plan, incorporating our strategy and transforming the way we work, they will in turn provide an opportunity for Partners to renew their own sense of purpose and affinity with the Partnership.

13

Real estate and the Covid-19 pandemic

SALLY HEMMING

Dr Sally Hemming is the Head of Wellbeing at Jones Lang LaSalle (JLL), a global real-estate services company employing over 90,000 workers across 80 countries, who buy, build, occupy and invest in various assets including industrial, commercial, retail, residential and hotel real estate.

'From this evening I must give the British people a very simple instruction – you must stay at home. Because the critical thing we must do is stop the disease spreading,' Boris Johnson, 23 March 2020.

In March 2020, the working world for UK workers changed as the country locked down in response to Covid-19, a novel and infectious disease caused by the coronavirus. People were instructed to leave home only for limited and essential reasons. While workers were able to travel to and from work, this was only if necessary and to undertake key work (eg nursing) or work not feasibly undertaken remotely. Concurrently, schools were closed to most children. Despite efforts to emerge from lockdown from June 2020, a second was imposed in the October followed by a tiered restrictions programme. At the time of writing, a promising vaccination scheme is being rolled out in the UK and Ireland (UKI); national restrictions remain in place and are being eased. Many workplaces remain closed.

A pandemic is a disease that spreads over a country or the world and it is difficult to predict when one will occur. Although employers' health and wellbeing approaches were gaining traction pre-pandemic, programmes focused on general health and lifestyle behaviours, avoiding chronic disease and mental health. For the first time in British history, the pandemic mandated employers to urgently adjust to and mitigate a communicable and indiscriminate disease risk. Consequently, many workers needed to embrace new and remote ways of working overnight. A best practice model for employers to follow did not exist. Nonetheless, employers have and continue to respond to changes originating from the pandemic's effects.

JLL is a global real-estate services company employing over 90,000 workers across 80 countries, who buy, build, occupy and invest in various assets including industrial, commercial, retail, residential and hotel real estate. From tech start-ups to global firms, clients span industries including banking, energy, healthcare, legal, manufacturing and technology. Unsurprisingly, the pandemic has raised questions about the sustainability of current ways of working, productivity, health and wellbeing, and the role and purpose of physical workspaces. While JLL helps clients navigate the pandemic's implications on their workplaces, it is also navigating its own challenges.

This chapter shares the narrative perspectives of JLL's senior leaders on the pandemic and predominately UKI including the organizational response and the pandemic's impacts, challenges, learning, and future thoughts. We hope that the narratives are thought-provoking and help inform organizational thinking and actions.

ANNE-SOPHIE CURET, EMEA HEAD OF PEOPLE AND SPACES
Impact and response

Within 24 hours of lockdown, we were forced to embrace new ways of working. This was coupled with very different levels of maturity and ability to engage with matters. We were in uncharted territory.

Furthermore, each country approached things differently and at different times, with people at different stages. So, while we were all in new and uncharted waters, there was not a playbook outlining what this meant. We started to think about our people and their families. Everything was up in the air.

As a global company we were fortunate to see things coming from Asia. Covid-19 hitting Italy was the starkest realization for us, and we started calling our Italian colleagues daily to ascertain the situation we were confronting. At this point, we contacted our IT teams to find out if we had the bandwidth for people across the globe to work remotely. The next week we forced a trial of remote working (including UKI) as a test and by the following week, most people were working from home. We had one drill test, which was amazing because JLL had the technology to support people. Instantly, we then started mapping our wellbeing roadmap and delivered our first wellbeing modules very quickly. We knew, for example, that managers needed guidance managing remote teams and that employees needed guidance about remote working. Moreover, while we are a large global company, at the same time, the crisis was handled locally. Each local situation was different, and authority was delegated to enable people to manage things locally as required. While it was unclear what might lay ahead, we knew we needed to reach people and ensure that they were ok.

People's experiences of lockdown varied. While some people felt home working relieved pressures, for others, including parents and carers, new and different pressures emerged. People were adjusting to working remotely, managing technology and other new arrangements. Some people rediscovered time with their families and enjoyed not commuting, whereas others experienced difficulties balancing home and work, were anxious and worried, and missed connecting with people. We surveyed people very quickly to ascertain their thinking and what they were up to, running thousands of surveys to understand where people were with their hearts and minds. This happened early on, week after week. We set up regular communications, were honest, and shared what we knew while accepting and being up-front about what we did not. It felt like there was a mix of pressure and joy.

Challenges and learning

We learnt that when people were working at home, without knowing it, we were managing people's home environment. We indirectly felt that sometimes we managed family dynamics and invaded people's private spaces whereas people normally leave work, get a train and go home. Because we had never experienced this, it was hard to rest; we constantly asked ourselves what we were missing or should be anticipating. We tried to be everywhere and all things but were sometimes limited in the measures we could take. We were concerned about the business impacts, our financial resilience and potential consequences from an employment perspective. Yet we were most concerned about fatalities. At the start, there was maybe one case we knew of, and things felt remote. Then, an employee or their family were affected, and circles felt narrower and the pandemic became very real. We asked ourselves, how do we create perspective for people and recreate a future with such ambiguity? How do we create a routine and perspective so that people re-engage and feel cared for? How do we help people continue to look after our clients?

We needed a new sense of urgency and to get people excited about the business and their jobs, so we worked to give people common goals and set objectives. This meant that some managers learnt how to be managers for the first time and had to figure out a way of addressing growth collectively and individually.

People's lives were suddenly on screen. We had moved into people's private spheres. Yet we found that people discovered emotions and started to speak more, sharing when they were feeling good or awful. People spoke more about their wellbeing and were accepting of others, which in turn accelerated our wellbeing agenda, making it a more common language. Yet the experiences of those workers required and allowed to work on client sites was different. Some people felt exposed and angry, perhaps because they had people at home with health conditions and were worried about this new virus and its effects. Daily we learnt something new that informed our ways of working and behaviour. Daily our behaviours were dictated by something unknown, with Covid-19 feeling like it was getting closer and closer.

We perceive that in the first lockdown people had more energy, solidarity and support. There is now more fatigue and people can be more self-interested. The absence of connection with colleagues presents work as a production activity and while people have tried to maintain connection with Teams drinks, for example, people have slowed down. Teams is associated more with work production than closeness. Additionally, while we know that we need to incorporate Covid-19 into our working lives and think and behave differently, we cannot always control things. The UKI experience was in some ways unique; in many other countries ambiguous events are more common (eg tornadoes) but the UKI is not often hit by these sorts of events. So, wellbeing is going to be at the centre of what we do for the future of all our people wherever they are, in order to enable resilience strategies.

We had started our wellbeing journey, but the pandemic has accelerated it, along with our technological approach. Projects that could have taken five years took two days and the managers' key role was reinforced. Lastly, we learnt about the importance of preparedness and our adaptability. Normally in large global companies you would have drills and audits for disruptive events but in the absence of readiness specifically for Covid-19, we successfully overcame significant challenges.

Future thoughts

Long Covid, with potential repeated cycles of illness, and people's mental health will be priorities for workplace support. As we were unable to recruit our usual graduate numbers, potentially creating talent gaps, we intend to embed an exciting graduate programme too. We will also work closely with those people who joined us during the pandemic, to understand their experiences and to secure their bond with the company. We are thinking ahead and planning for what comes next. We realize that after major crises people can recover, potentially relieved but also exhausted. People have been confronted with situations they had no experience of. For some it has been overwhelming, with life continuing to happen round them, including births, deaths and divorces. No one quite knows how to recover. While some things are unclear, we are finding ways to revive the drive and success in our people by supporting them.

We have realized our role as an employer is reflected in the way we support our workers. We continue to pay people, aid home working, and accept that if people cannot concentrate, that is ok. We are taking practical measures and not just wellbeing interventions, to make people's lives better despite what they are going through. The ways we are behaving in any given country, starting with the senior leadership, are extremely caring and generous. It has really been about our people and clients. We have looked after our people and will continue to improve on our ways of working, and create spaces that are clean, welcoming and work for our people and clients, both now and in the future.

JAMES ADDISON, UK HEAD OF OPERATIONS
Impact and response

23 March 2020 is cemented in my mind. Specifically, we had run a test shutdown of our UK office sites on 13 March with no technology issues, which is testament to our IT teams. London never came out of that and the next week all regional sites closed. We have been in and out of lockdowns since, opening offices whenever we could. For lockdowns three and four we kept offices open, particularly from a health and wellbeing perspective. For example, not everyone had a suitable workspace at home and we needed space for people working on client site.

We enacted a planned emergency response approach and responded to people's support needs. While not planned on such a scale, having an emergency response was valuable. We had also previously undergone a restructure, establishing national business lines which then served to build a sense of community and an expanded senior leadership team. This team met twice-weekly, providing clear Covid-19 messaging to business lines, thus reducing communication channels. In parallel, a small tiger team originated pandemic-relevant policies and governed measures including our Covid-secure practices, wellbeing support, home working set-ups, and our response to the furlough initiative. Alongside this, it became more important to support established networks for working parents and diversity. Working parents suffered most, particularly those who did not have support bubbles. It was an unbelievably difficult time and many people felt that they were not winning in either role. The network provided great support, but we wonder what more we could have done – something to reflect on.

Like almost all professional services businesses, the pandemic's main impact has been on our movement to structured Teams meetings in place of unstructured face-to-face interactions, resulting in increased working hours for many. As the majority continue to work from home, those coming into the office are spending significant time on Teams rather than face to face. We will need to find a balance as hybrid working becomes a part of our day-to-day lives. We have become used to working during our commute time, so working days have naturally extended, a pace at which we have learnt to work, but which again needs to be rebalanced as we emerge from Covid. We advised safeguards for our people to help mitigate this – moving to walking meetings, reducing to 25- or 50-minute meetings to enable breaks, encouraging daily exercise and free Headspace subscriptions. Yet despite these safeguards, we have been largely home-based and with nowhere else to go, and the boundaries between work and home seem to have evaporated. Without fixed breaks away from home (and sunnier climates) we have not achieved separation.

Burn-out has been a real risk throughout the pandemic. That being said, the increased flexibility this new way of working has offered in terms of supporting families and removing dependency on five-day office working, has been hugely positive. We managed to achieve outstanding results despite the complete move to remote working. Now as we return to offices, even in a hybrid capacity, we need to rebalance, retaining the best of both face-to-face collaboration and increased flexibility. Our perspectives are changing.

The pandemic has accelerated our technological and flexible working approaches. We do not envisage people working in the office 9 to 5 or travelling to the extent that they once did. It has been more than a year, and some will find it inconceivable to return to the office soon. The pandemic threw into focus ways of working that we might not have entertained. As a traditional industry, while we aspired to technological change, it has been a journey. Teams could not envisage winning or executing mandates unless face to face. We have been forced to accelerate in terms of how we work, probably by five years or more. We would never have seen acceptance of collaboration tools at the rate we have had to in such a short period. We have been surprised by our achievements and the subsequent benefits.

Challenges and learning

At the time, competitors came together to form an operations group to ensure shared approaches and aid interpretation of government guidelines. Having to navigate changing guidelines that were not sector-specific, and with little steer, was challenging. We felt we were to-ing and fro-ing, erring on the right side of the guidance and caution. That balance of interpretation, government guidance, keeping people safe and preparing the workplace was difficult. Additional to safeguarding our people, we had to safeguard our business. Not knowing the impact of Covid-19 early in the pandemic, we took cost actions throughout 2020, which we have since largely reversed. In hindsight we could have taken a more risk-based approach; however, we had to take fiscally responsible actions in those unprecedented times.

We learnt that people's health was an absolute priority. The past year has put concerns about individual and corporate wellbeing and mitigating infection risks centre stage. Not all lessons are yet learnt because we are still facing into things. However, we need to think back to how we used to operate and return to taking breaks, holidays and switching off. Moreover, and on reflection, in the first lockdown we did not prepare ourselves for how long it could be. We worked to the next government guidelines evolving at two- to three-week intervals and towards 'unlocking'. We worked in hope but now wonder if we should have taken a longer-term view. Although we were trying to remain in lockstep with the government, providing fortnightly updates to our people, we might have read this differently.

What helped us most was our level of communication – as an operational team, as a leadership team and as managers with our direct reports. Always front of mind when forming our response policies and protocols were the needs of the business and how we would communicate – through townhalls, emails, playbooks, landing sites and briefing materials. One of the silver linings of the pandemic is the way in which it brought teams closer together as we sought to over-communicate to ensure one another's wellbeing. This is something we will continue.

We envisage challenges returning to the office. While we have office capacity and follow government safety guidelines, it will be challenging getting people to return, but we will encourage it when we can, and will remove barriers. Yet if we look at our workplace surveys, people want to spend about 50 per cent of working time at home. How we manage that from a workplace standpoint, so that we do not have everyone coming into the office Tuesday, Wednesday and Thursday, needs thought. People have new lives now, and different expectations and commitments they need to balance with work. We want to offer this flexibility while also doing what we can to encourage people back. We continue to see tremendous value in the office, but as a space for collaboration, team working and creative thinking: moments that matter.

Until people come back to the office, the mental health and wellbeing boost it can offer is hard to describe. For example, despite meeting calls you also have time to catch up with people and socialize; for some, the boost of face-to-face meetings can be unbelievable. We see value in interaction and in serendipitous encounters. It is amazing how much creativity and business you can generate by asking peers what is keeping them busy and discussing it. These things do not happen on Teams, and our one JLL culture is challenged when you must formally arrange them. The value of chance encounters and potential wellbeing boosts are aspects that we hope will encourage people to return to offices.

Future thoughts

Managing a business and cost impacts when you are unclear what lies ahead is challenging. We need to consider our operating model, which is at the forefront of our minds. We envisage hard work helping our workers to have confidence and balance through events, top-down leadership, office set-ups, and working through flexible schemes (to achieve self-managing teams). We need to consider what our people tell us and how we operate in a new normal, right down to the level of the cost of train travel! As things change and move away from government policy, there will be all sorts of things to consider. People will continue to perform and communicate output, sharing what works for them or otherwise. We trust our people. The real challenge is taking those insights and weaving them into our approach.

14

Legal sector
and the Covid-19 pandemic

SUZANNE HORNE

Suzanne Horne is a Partner and Vice-Chair of the London Office of Paul Hastings LLP (the 'Firm'), one of the leading law firms in the world, with 21 global offices across Europe, Asia, Latin America and the United States and circa 1,600 employees. Our #1 goal is to consistently deliver exceptional service to our clients wherever they are in the world. We seek to achieve this by navigating new paths to growth for our clients, our people, and the world around us. This drives our growth strategy, our talent strategy, our collaborative culture and our values.

With offices in Beijing, Hong Kong, Seoul, Shanghai and Tokyo, we experienced the start of what would transpire to be a global pandemic in early 2020. Our offices in Asia closed their doors and our colleagues were the first to experience the remote working that was soon to become the 'norm', so to speak, for all of us. At that time, comparisons were drawn to SARs and Avian flu and with this came an expectation that we in Europe and the United States would remain largely unaffected. However, our experience as a Firm in Asia in those early months of 2020 allowed us the opportunity to navigate the challenges thrown up by Covid-19 for five offices first, and with it the chance to think through and implement the contingency plans for the rest of the Firm. For some time, we monitored the ongoing escalation and its impact on all aspects of business and operations with increasing trepidation, but by late February we were all seeing the virus ravage Italy and it was becoming increasingly apparent that it was just a matter of time before it spread across Europe and to the United States, even if no one could foresee the full extent of the crisis.

By early March 2020, the decision had been taken not to gather Firm management, partners and clients for the annual meeting. The powerful 'tone from the top' was that the health and wellbeing of the entire Paul Hastings community is paramount, and it was not appropriate to put that at risk if there was even a small chance of adding to infection rates. This proved to be the consistent theme of communications and messaging for the next 12 months. It united staff and lawyers, and proved invaluable in achieving the other primary consideration in planning and decision making – how to provide uninterrupted service to our clients.

As we navigated the uncertainties in our personal and professional lives, the Firm set up a Covid-19 task force to centrally manage and respond to the situation, which was developing with extraordinary speed. Memos were drafted, preparations were made, meetings cancelled, non-essential travel stopped, and the robustness and security of the mobile technology infrastructure were tested. The Firm's pre-Covid planned roll-out of Webex was suddenly embraced like a long-lost relative as we craved visual interaction with each other and our clients. This was a significant change to the usual method of communication used by most of the legal profession at that time of conference calls with multiple participants, and 'who just joined' quickly became 'you are on mute'. Come mid-March 2020, it was officially a global pandemic and the 'stay home' announcement was made for the entire Firm. In the end, the transition to remote working was relatively seamless. Shortly thereafter, the word 'unprecedented' became overused.

Over the next 15 months we saw the crisis present an array of challenges that tested our strength and resilience, and shone a bright light on the health, safety and wellbeing of all our colleagues and their families like never before. I set out below how we responded to the crisis and some of the practical steps that we took to manage health and wellbeing for our colleagues in a high-performing professional services environment.

Strong Firm leadership

Our management of health and wellbeing started with communications from the very top of our Firm. We received regular updates from Firm and office management as the impacts of the pandemic unfolded, communicated on video conferences, by telephone and by email. Firm management did not furlough vast swathes of lawyers and professional staff like others in the legal profession. It stood firm and confident – there were no mass redundancies or knee-jerk pay cuts – and in doing so undoubtedly alleviated another potential source of stress and anxiety that some experienced during the crisis.

In preparing this chapter, I have re-read some of the contemporaneous written communications and I am struck by the words used, sent in the grip of a crisis that seemed unmanageable for so long. They convey information, plans and results, but they also motivate and reassure; they emphasize the importance of the health and wellbeing of the entire Paul Hastings community, acknowledging the challenges faced by all of us, and they reiterate time and time again the importance for partners, managers and team leaders to connect, reach out and engage with their teams and our clients.

Alongside these management communications, the Firm leveraged some existing initiatives, platforms and programming, and devised some incredible new initiatives and support during a tumultuous period.

Mental health awareness and the Mindful Business Charter at Paul Hastings

As a Firm we had become increasingly aware over the last five to ten years of the issues of mental health and wellbeing in the legal profession and, as set out in further detail below, had already started our journey to help address some of these issues. We mark US Mental

Illness Awareness Week and the UK's Mental Health Awareness Week, and pre-Covid, we held a series of locally led initiatives including hosted meditation classes and yoga sessions, offering healthy and convenient food, compiling a local wellness library and talks on mental health in the legal profession. In light of the crisis, these local interactions went online.

In addition to this general awareness, the Firm is also a signatory to the Mindful Business Charter, originally devised by Barclays Bank plc and some of its panel law firms to address mindfulness and well-being. It aims to promote best practices for a healthy work environment, where there are times when long hours and stress cannot be avoided. While originally focused on financial services and the legal profession, it is now aimed at the business community at large. The Charter sets out practical advice on how to embed its core principles of Openness and Respect, Respecting Rest Periods, Smart Meetings and Emails, and Mindful Delegation to practise mindful business. In the US, the Firm is also a signatory to the American Bar Association's Wellbeing Pledge. These tools are not a silver bullet, and we recognize that more needs to be done to address the challenges we face as a Firm and as a profession, but as referenced below, that is the next chapter in our health and wellbeing story.

PH Balanced

In addition to leveraging this general awareness, the Firm drew on its PH Balanced initiative. Launched in 2017, PH Balanced seeks to redefine Big Law culture by bringing together people from across the Firm – lawyers, professional staff, and management – to discuss shared challenges to achieving greater balance. In 2018, with the recent increased awareness in the legal industry around issues such as stress management and mental wellbeing, the PH Balanced Committee narrowed their programming to directly address this increasing need.

Programming includes global and local options focused on family and parental topics, work/life balance, mindfulness, mental health, stress management and wellness-type activities and discussions. During the crisis, it has been the perfect banner for regular communications, with tips and resources on staying well emotionally, physically and socially, from exercises to recipes, working remotely, family care, webinars by our wellness, yoga and meditation provider, coping with stress, and emergency kits for anxiety, worry and stress. It also highlighted the broad range of employee benefits, including various different types of leave, whether for personal or family-friendly reasons, including a policy of unlimited time off for our lawyers.

PH Balanced leadership also instigated Mindful Thursdays, a short 15-minute meditation session with a certified mindfulness facilitator, who also happens to be our Director of PR and Communications at the Firm. They also held a series of talks, 'Staying Positive and Working from Home Effectively: the Rules by Sir Cary Cooper', 'Substance Use and Mental Health Disorders', 'Psychological Fortitude: More Than Mental Health and Coping Strategies During a Race-related Crisis', and discussions with partners and professional staff who shared tips on trying to build resilience in a pandemic. These sessions (combined with other DE&I programming) addressed not only the issues of health and wellbeing during the crisis but also racial injustice, the killing of George Floyd and the Black Lives Matter protests and movement. After all, the global pandemic did not happen in a vacuum.

PH Balanced has subsequently received external recognition and Paul Hastings was a finalist for Mental Health & Wellbeing (Law Firm) at the UK Diversity Legal Awards 2020.

EAP, counselling and access to therapy

All Paul Hastings employees are entitled to private medical insurance cover as an employee benefit but one of the resources repeatedly flagged in the monthly PH Balanced newsletters sent during the crisis is access to the Employee Assistance Program (EAP). This confidential resource helps colleagues deal with life's challenges and the demands that come with balancing home and work. It provides confidential, professional referrals and up to five sessions of face-to-face counselling for a wide variety of concerns. It also gives our colleagues access to a digital guided therapy programme that supports them in making long-term personal change. It is a service provided by a third-party organization of healthcare professionals. It is paid for by the Firm but the Firm is not made aware of who uses it, or what is discussed. Therefore, it is difficult to gain any real visibility on how much or how little this resource was utilized during the crisis across the jurisdictions, but I do believe that it was a valuable tool for some who needed more than line manager support or financial assistance.

Covid hardship fund

In April 2020, early on in the crisis, the Firm launched a special fund for employees and their immediate family members and dependents who were experiencing financial hardships from both the direct and indirect impacts of Covid-19. The concept of the fund arose from Firm leadership reaching out to chairs of the PH Balanced Committee who wanted to discuss the most pressing issues facing our colleagues. The team recognized that some of our PH colleagues were experiencing unexpected financial burdens from the pandemic, such as increased medical-related expenses, the loss of a partner's, dependent's or roommate's income, increased utility bills, or having college-age students back at home. This gave rise to the creation of the Paul Hastings Covid-19 Fund. Partners, lawyers and professional staff were given the opportunity to make contributions to the fund and the Firm matched donations. The Firm also made additional contributions to the fund on annual Administrative Professionals day. This is a day when the Firm and its lawyers have traditionally given a small gift or put on a lunch by way of a token of appreciation for the professional staff that help make our Firm so successful.

Those facing challenging financial circumstances were encouraged to apply. The only criteria and prioritization was on the basis of need as assessed by the PH Balanced Committee – not office, position or seniority. This initiative was born out of a belief that we support each other at difficult times and that we are better off facing unprecedented circumstances together.

Home equipment and technology support

As well as crucial financial support for those facing financial hardship, in the immediate transition to remote work the Firm also rallied around those who needed relatively simple things, like chairs with the appropriate lumbar support. But by April, it introduced a formal programme that enabled employees to easily buy and be reimbursed for technology equipment for use at home that was compatible with Firm systems.

A shift in the focus of wellbeing

During the course of 2020, in accordance with the then UK Government guidance, the London office complied with all the requirements to create a Covid-secure workplace and we started a phased reopening for those who could not work effectively from home. Like so many organizations, some colleagues live alone, some share flats where there isn't a dedicated workspace or equipment, and some needed to redefine the divide between home and work for their own wellbeing. Having spent such considerable time focusing on physical health and wellbeing and the risks of contracting Covid-19, we rightly saw a redress of the balance to also acknowledge the mental toll colleagues were experiencing from isolation and remoteness during the crisis. In going to the office at this time, there was a wonderful camaraderie and warmth from seeing colleagues again on what felt like the other side of the crisis. While it was relatively short-lived before the further lockdown at the end of 2020, it was a welcome reminder of the sense of community, value of human and social interaction, and common purpose that form an integral part of our culture as a Firm.

The return to work

We are now looking forward to the reopening of all of our global offices. Firm management has announced that as of the beginning of September, all team members – both lawyers and professional staff –

should be working from the office. In doing so, the Firm has brought certainty to another period of potential uncertainty, stress and anxiety, as to what the return to work will mean for the PH community and our Firm. That said, there is understanding and respect for the flexibility that individual circumstances will require, even if, by default, we should work from the office when we are able. This return to office is as important for helping to nurture and strengthen our sense of culture, teamwork and collaboration as it is for serving clients at the highest levels and, ultimately, is consistent with our #1 goal.

Conclusions

As we all start to properly emerge from this crisis, the initiatives, programming and support for the health and wellbeing of our employees have clearly held us in good stead; the Firm has had the most successful quarter in its history and has recognized the incredible contribution made by all lawyers and professional staff during the crisis. However, we are not complacent; there is much work still to do. All of the surveys of the legal profession indicate an ongoing problem with health and wellbeing. For example, just last month, a survey published by Patrick Krill and psychologist Justin Anker of the University of Minnesota Medical School found that 25 per cent of women lawyers surveyed in 2020 said that they were considering leaving the legal profession because of mental health issues, burnout and stress (Spiezio, 2021). At the time of writing (March 2021), further headlines in the legal press referred to 'Associate Burn-Out is Real: Firms Can and Must Do More' (Offomata, 2021). Therefore, while we as a Firm may have navigated what we hope is the worst of the pandemic, and coped admirably with the unprecedented crisis, we now have to get down to the business of managing workplace health and wellbeing coming out of the crisis and beyond. And, to quote the Mindful Business Charter, 'Be Brave'.

References

Offomata, A (2021) Associate burn-out is real: 'firms can and must do more', https://www.law.com/international-edition/2021/06/03/associate-burn-out-is-real-firms-can-and-must-do-more/ (archived at https://perma.cc/4W74-E7BJ)

Spiezio, C (2021) Mental health, stress have one-in-four women lawyers mulling career change, https://www.reuters.com/business/legal/mental-health-stress-have-one-in-four-women-lawyers-mulling-career-change-2021-05-12/ (archived at https://perma.cc/KX2B-2HEL)

15

Professional services

Mind the manager wellbeing gap

CHARLES ALBERTS

Charles Alberts is the head of wellbeing solutions at Aon plc, an Irish-registered multinational professional services firm that sells a range of financial risk-mitigation products, including insurance, pension administration, and health insurance plans. Aon has approximately 50,000 employees in 120 countries. Here, Charles poses the question, 'Managers play a vital role in businesses and have been at the forefront of the response to the pandemic, but are we doing enough to protect their wellbeing?'

The Covid-19 pandemic has accelerated many trends that are likely to have a lasting impact – for many communicating via video has become the norm, and with a taste of working in a more agile way to balance work and home life it's an expectation that employees will demand greater flexibility from their employers. Even in roles where employees' work lives have seen little change through the pandemic, a door has been opened, with employers engaging in more open communications and on topics such as mental health, which may previously have been taboo.

We've also seen a greater focus on the role of managers and what's expected of them. Managers have needed to step up during the pandemic, connect with their teams on a personal level, understand what's going on in their lives, offer flexibility wherever possible, and often also provide emotional support by offering a compassionate, non-judgemental listening ear. Research by Lifeworks (2021) found that four out of every five managers have dealt with a specific mental health issue with at least one employee since the start of the pandemic.

However, this new approach to management won't have come naturally for a large cohort of hardened managers with a more dated approach to leadership, and many would have missed the mark. As one example, 55 per cent of managers report that they were not sure what to do when dealing with employee mental health (Lifeworks, 2021).

For some time now there's been an acknowledgement of the need to shift the model of promoting people who are good technically into management roles, which requires an entirely different skillset.

There is a sense that expectations of managers are now changing at pace. More than half (58 per cent) of managers believe their roles have significantly changed since the start of the pandemic and of these, 67 per cent see this change as enduring. Worryingly, more than one in four (28 per cent) don't feel confident in their ability to meet these new job expectations and four in ten felt they did not have support for key challenges such as additional duties, employee mental health, employee concerns about job security etc. This lack of confidence and ability is detrimental not only to the manager, but also to their team members.

Good managers have leadership, collaboration and communication skills that help create workforce resilience – vital when considering the top wellbeing risks impacting company performance, which are stress (67 per cent), burnout (46 per cent) and anxiety (37 per cent) as identified in Aon's 2021 Global Wellbeing Survey.

Managers help to manage these risks and in doing so increase organizational performance, yet CIPD's 2019 Health and Wellbeing at Work study found that after heavy workloads, management style was the second most frequently cited cause of stress, with a greater number of organizations citing this among their top three causes of work-related stress. So this is a two-sided coin.

Whatever conclusions can be drawn from this, managers are at the heart of business and it is imperative to ensure they have the right knowledge, skill and confidence to support their teams while protecting and enhancing their own wellbeing and resilience.

Aon's 2020 Rising Resilient study found that managers who themselves are resilient, with traits like mental endurance, learnability and empowerment, increase job performance by 20 per cent. Yet through the pandemic a worrying picture is starting to develop when it comes to the wellbeing of managers.

As people and employees themselves, managers have had to contend with the same changes, added pressures and disruption to their work and personal lives during the pandemic as everyone else. Already considered the 'squeezed middle' due to often conflicting demands from the business and their teams, they have faced additional pressures leading through an unprecedented period of uncertainty while ensuring business continuity and supporting their teams at the same time.

It's no surprise that managers' wellbeing has suffered as a result.

Research by Lifeworks published in April 2021 highlighted that levels of stress are becoming unbearable. Almost half of managers (44 per cent vs 28 per cent of non-managers) had considered leaving their role since the start of the pandemic; the main reason is stress at work (56 per cent of managers vs 48 per cent of non-managers) followed by stress in their personal life (32 per cent of managers vs 24 per cent of non-managers).

Bupa Global Executive Wellbeing Index found that nearly eight in ten (78 per cent) have experienced symptoms such as fatigue, lack of motivation, mood swings and disturbed sleep, and 64 per cent of senior business leaders who have experienced symptoms of mental ill-health during the pandemic have turned to potentially unhealthy coping mechanisms such as drugs and alcohol.

Mental health stigma is a particular concern and is higher among managers, perhaps because they perceive a requirement to always be resilient, strong and the ones others can depend on. Lifeworks' research found that nearly half (45 per cent of managers vs 38 per cent of non-managers) report that they would feel negatively about themselves if they had a mental health issue and more than half (54 per cent of managers vs 42 per cent of non-managers) perceive that there would be an impact to their career if their employer knew of a mental health issue. Bupa Global Executive Wellbeing Index had similar findings: two in five board executives (42 per cent) said they believed it would damage their reputation if it became known they were struggling.

Stigma itself is a risk factor for mental health as it can result in people delaying seeking support, and can increase feelings of isolation and additional pressure from not being able to be honest about how they are feeling. Out of all roles, managers consistently take the least number of sickness absence days in any given year (Office for National Statistics, 2020). This may be indicative of higher levels of stigma in this group, where presenteeism is therefore likely to be greater.

What can be done?

Promote right. From the very outset we need to rethink how we select people for managerial roles. This could include technical competencies but in view of the requirements of the modern leader, should be weighted towards personal and people management capabilities. We still need to recognize, retain and promote people who are technically strong and therefore require technical career paths where being promoted to a manager isn't the only career trajectory available.

Clarify expectations. While the pandemic has no doubt accelerated the trend towards contemporary expectations of the manager's role, now is the time to clearly articulate exactly what that is to remove any guesswork and provide a template against which to assess managers' current skills.

For instance, research by Business in the Community (2020) showed that 42 per cent of managers don't recognize providing mental health support to their team as part of their role. Unless issues such as mental health become an unquestionable part of each and every manager's role, we won't make the progress we need to in this area.

Training. Managers will all have different aptitudes, knowledge, skills, confidence and levels of experience. A skills gap analysis will help to identify the areas that specific managers need to work on, and can be used to create a tailored training programme. Investing in the development of managers will pay dividends for years to come, as identified in numerous studies including Bloom et al (2012).

For instance, in 2013 the UK Commission for Employment and Skills (UKCES) found that the five skills managers most lacked were strategic management, planning and organization, teamwork, problem solving, and oral communication. No doubt if this research was conducted today, the ability to support mental health and softer skills such as compassion and empathy would feature.

Much more needs to be done here – a third of organizations responding to this research stated that their managers had not received any training in the previous year or, if they had been trained, had not had the opportunity to implement what they had learnt.

Continued professional development. In addition to theoretical knowledge, managers build and refine their skills through practical on-the-job learning over time; first-hand experience is invaluable. To optimize the benefits from on-the-job learning this needs to be built in as a component of a CPD programme, alongside informal and more structured formal training. Initiating a mentoring programme where developing managers can share their experiences and obtain guidance from more experienced managers can be valuable not only in enhancing learning but can help to protect the wellbeing of the developing manager.

Support. For managers to be effective and to protect their wellbeing, they need support from a wide range of people – peers, their manager, HR, Employee Relations, etc – plus external benefits and services.

The support required is varied and will change for each manager over time and depending on the specific issue(s) they are dealing with. To establish this infrastructure consider, for instance, a peer network for managers to share experiences and test approaches, pairing developing managers with more experienced HR professionals, with a debrief as standard on any emotionally challenging situations or discussions (not dissimilar to supervision in a clinical environment), and a practical guide to external benefits and services such as an Employee Assistance Programme or Occupational Health, when these should be used and how they benefit the manager.

Role models. With high levels of stigma around issues such as mental health, struggling to cope, being impacted by difficult situations etc, it's vital that we encourage more managers as role models who are willing to open up and honestly talk about their experiences – good and bad. Sharing experiences can be impactful in reducing feelings of isolation and inadequacy to protect managers' wellbeing.

Monitor and manage pressure. Managers' roles are varied, ambiguous at times, boundaries blurred, subject to conflicting priorities, varied numbers of people reporting to them, and with ultimate responsibility that they can feel forced to pick up additional work that can't be accommodated in the team, leading to additional pressure. Combined with not always feeling equipped to manage the expectations of them, this can lead to unmanageable levels of pressure, stress and ultimately burnout. It is imperative that businesses regularly monitor the pressure managers are under and take proactive action to protect their wellbeing. With unmanageable pressures managers could neglect the 'people management' aspects of their role, which could have a detrimental impact on their teams also.

What has Aon done?

At Aon we are driven to empower economic and human possibility for clients, colleagues and communities around the world. We are a leading global professional services firm providing a broad range of risk, retirement and health solutions. Our 50,000 colleagues in 120 countries empower results for clients by using proprietary data and analytics to deliver insights that reduce volatility and improve performance.

Aon has taken a broad global, regional and local approach to developing and supporting its people leaders. With over 1,000 managers in the UK, a number have undertaken formal studies and have gained diplomas from the Chartered Management Institute, and the first cohort of MSc students are currently completing their leadership studies. In addition to professional studies, Aon offers a wide range of personal, professional and leadership development programmes internally and has established a leadership development pathway to guide managers through their development. Here managers can select from a wide range of individual courses or attend a complete programme. The content ranges from mental health awareness and stress management, to leading virtual teams, inclusion studies, unconscious bias training for hiring managers, bringing your best, and countless others.

A range of tools and resources including reference guides are available and regular workshops are held on pertinent topics such as looking after your own and your team's wellbeing during the winter months. Aon shares a regular newsletter dedicated to managers, which includes key information they need to know together with leadership development content.

For the practical requirements of a manager's role, Aon provides step-by-step guidance on issues such as onboarding new colleagues, holding personal development discussions with their teams, holding performance review discussions, and others.

The firm has a formal mentoring programme where managers are actively encouraged to mentor others and have a mentor themselves.

Ultimately, it's managers' engagement with the development and support that's provided and the resulting impact on them and their teams that's most important. This is monitored in various ways which, combined with input on what would be valuable, informs the most impactful ways to continually evolve the firm's approach.

Closing thoughts

Through the pandemic, businesses everywhere have relied on their managers to step up like never before. Managers play a vital role in businesses, delivering results through effective leadership, operations and people management. Increasingly it's the modern, professional manager with good leadership, communication, engagement and soft skills who's in demand.

However, added pressure, patchy training and a lack of support are having a detrimental impact on the health and wellbeing of managers. We need managers to be their best if we expect them to help their teams be the best. Change is required to protect and enhance the wellbeing of our managers – it's an oversight we can no longer afford.

References

Aon (2020) The Rising Resilient, https://www.aon.com/risingresilient/ (archived at https://perma.cc/H2W2-U78H)

Aon (2021) Global Wellbeing Survey, https://www.aon.com/global-wellbeing-survey.aspx (archived at https://perma.cc/JEF8-F959)

Bloom, N et al (2012) Management practices across firms and countries, *Academy of Management Perspectives*, 26, pp 12–33, https://journals.aom.org/doi/abs/10.5465/amp.2011.0077 (archived at https://perma.cc/J3VN-X5KG)

Bupa (2020) Global Executive Wellbeing Index, https://www.covermagazine.co.uk/news/4023684/business-leaders-self-medicating-mental-health-issues (archived at https://perma.cc/DKX3-8WF5)

Business in the Community (2020) Mental Health at Work, https://www.bitc.org.uk/fact-sheet/mental-health-at-work-2020-infographic/ (archived at https://perma.cc/QW6W-VTHH)

CIPD (2019) Health and Well-being at Work, https://www.cipd.co.uk/knowledge/culture/well-being/health-well-being-work#gref (archived at https://perma.cc/2WBY-GVR5) (see survey archive). Direct link to report: https://www.cipd.co.uk/Images/health-and-well-being-at-work-2019.v1_tcm18-55881.pdf (archived at https://perma.cc/5KLC-5S88)

Lifeworks (2021) Mental health for people leaders during COVID-19: Leading on the edge, https://lifeworks.com/en/resource/mental-health-people-leaders-during-covid-19-leading-edge (archived at https://perma.cc/3XCB-QKCE)

Office for National Statistics (2020) Sickness absence in the UK labour market: 2020, Figure 8: Elementary occupations are the only group seeing an increase in sickness absence over the decade, https://www.ons.gov.uk/employmentandlabourmarket/peopleinwork/labourproductivity/articles/sicknessabsenceinthelabourmarket/2020 (archived at https://perma.cc/SG7L-K2GH)

UK Commission For Employment And Skills (2013) Management matters: Key findings from the UKCES surveys, London: UKCES, https://www.voced.edu.au/content/ngv%3A57665 (archived at https://perma.cc/F4E5-JFJH)

16

Health

Impact of Covid on the older worker – an early view

CAROL BLACK
PAUL LITCHFIELD
KAREN SANCTO
RICHARD CADDIS
TONY VICKERS-BYRNE

This short review, originally written for a round-table discussion in December 2020, encompasses the earlier part of the pandemic, before the introduction of vaccination.

Prior to Covid

In the years prior to the Covid-19 pandemic the increase in total UK employment was in large part driven by increase in the number of over-50s in work. This accounted for three-quarters of the increase in people in work between 2004 and 2019. However, much of this additional work has been of an insecure nature: low-paid, temporary or self-employed. For people in work, this work was insecure for 10 per cent of the 55–64-year-olds, and for 20 per cent of 65–74-year-olds. The gap in numbers of employed between those aged 50–64 and those aged 35– 49 stood at 12.8 percentage points in 2019, and it is estimated that around 1 million people aged between 50 and the state pension age were not working but would have liked to be.

Forecasts had looked good for the older worker, as shown for example in Mercer's Workforce Monitor for March 2018 (www.uk. mercer.com), which predicted that after seven years there would be 300,000 fewer workers under the age of 30 in the UK, but 1 million more workers aged over 50.

The pandemic has come like a whirlwind, drastically changed this, and as can be shown, has made employment prospects much worse for the older worker.

Covid and age

At the start of the pandemic, both in Asia and Europe, an increased severity and fatality rate from Covid was evident. This was seen in the initial weeks in the UK, but was focused on the very elderly (aged), with significant pre-existing health conditions and residing in care home facilities. Deaths have continued to be highest in those 80 years of age and older (49 per cent); the median age of the fatal cases was 80 years (IQR 71–86). Since September, 3,581 cases were hospitalized (3.6 per cent of all reported cases), with a median age of 60 years (IQR 41–74). Therefore the risk from the hazard that is Covid-19 is present, and will be with us for some time, and therefore needs to be considered carefully against prolonged protection and/or absence from the workplace and society.

Hazard and risk

We are better prepared now in terms of diagnosis, with increased and targeted testing, clearer understanding of the most effective methods of track, trace and isolate, and advances in medical management and treatment protocols (such as the use of steroids to reduce the need for mechanical ventilation – one of the key indicators of significant adverse outcome).

The risk to the older worker of being and staying out of gainful employment will have significant physical, psychological, social and welfare impacts in the coming 12 months.

We are now at the start of a second, albeit less draconian, lockdown, but we must look forward to what a considered and balanced return to work would look like, with appropriate, reasonable, achievable and effective controls in place to allow the older worker to be in work, undertake meaningful and gainful employment, and remain part of wider society. The critical issue is whether there are jobs for them to remain in or return to after furloughing (now extended to end March 2021), or whether we will see the older worker excluded from the workplace, so that age becomes a fracture line in our society.

Unemployment

The effects of the pandemic are multiple and complex, but perhaps after the dreadful loss of life one of the most visible effects in the first few months of the pandemic was the rise in unemployment.

Analysis by IES of Bank of England and Office for National Statistics labour force surveys shows the rise in claimant count for unemployment benefit to be the fastest since the system was set up in 1922 – the count has doubled for all age groups (Figures 16.1 and 16.2).

Unemployment is one of the most damaging factors affecting personal wellbeing, its impact going well beyond the effects of reduced income. Asked whether they felt life is 'worthwhile', almost 10 per cent of unemployed people reported a low level (0–4 on an 11-point scale), compared with just over 2 per cent in the employed population (ONS data 2012–15).

Work is generally good for both physical and mental health and wellbeing. Work needs to be 'good work' which is healthy, safe and offers some autonomy so as to build a sense of self-worth. Social contact, time structure, status, purpose and identity are other essential experiences that a worker gets from paid employment – all of these factors relate to wellbeing. Overall, the beneficial effects of

FIGURE 16.1 Unemployment claims over the past century

Administrative and claimant unemployment, 1922-present

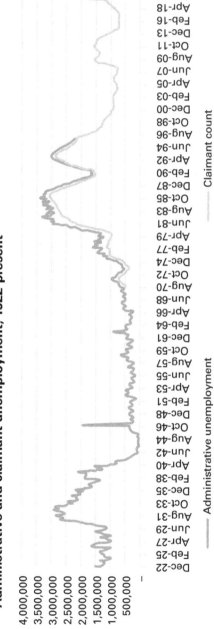

Administrative unemployment ———   Claimant count ———

FIGURE 16.1 (Continued)

Year-on-year change in administrative/claimant unemployment, 1922-present

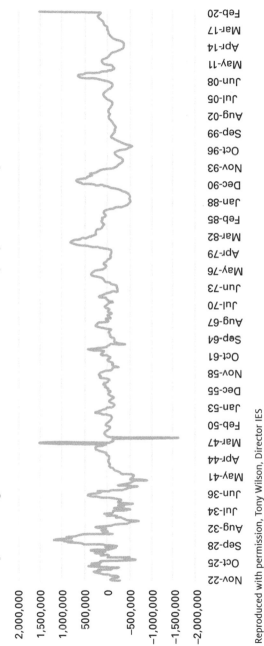

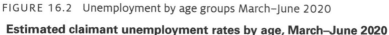

FIGURE 16.2   Unemployment by age groups March–June 2020

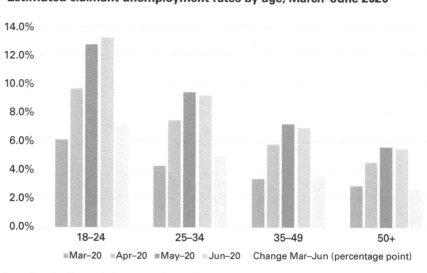

Estimated claimant unemployment rates by age, March–June 2020

Reproduced with permission, Tony Wilson, Director IES

work far outweigh the risks involved, and are much greater than the harmful effects of long-term worklessness. A large mental health deficit is associated with unemployment and physical inactivity; this applies to the older worker as much as the younger one.

For the older worker, those who lose their jobs are far more likely to slip into long-term worklessness. Just one in three (35 per cent) over-50s who lose their job return to work quickly, compared to two in three (63 per cent) workers aged 25–34. Over-50s who are unemployed are twice as likely as those aged 18–24 to have been out of work for over a year.

Over-50s have been poorly served by previous employment support programmes. The Work Programme – which was introduced following the last recession – failed older claimants; just 19 per cent of adults in their late 50s found a lasting job, compared to 38 per cent of young people aged 18–24.

These results do not cover workers aged 65 or over, but the official Labour Force Survey data certainly do, and give yet more cause for concern. Employment levels for those aged 65 or over were 105,000 lower in June–August 2020 than six months earlier, a fall of 7.5 per

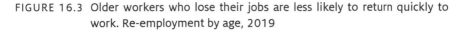

FIGURE 16.3 Older workers who lose their jobs are less likely to return quickly to work. Re-employment by age, 2019

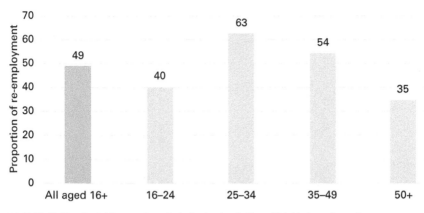

SOURCE NatCen Social Research analysis for Ageing Better, official Labour Force Survey

cent, taking the employment rate down from 11.5 per cent to 10.5 per cent. Overall this group, despite making up only 4 per cent of the workforce, has accounted for one-fifth (21 per cent) of the total fall in employment during the crisis. Young people have been similarly affected, with employment of under-25s also falling by 7.5 per cent over those six months. However, for younger people this increase has been offset by significant increases in numbers in full-time education.

The Resolution Foundation's report 'The Full Monty' (see Figure 16.4) found that one in ten 18–24 year olds had lost their main job, more than double the 4 per cent average across all age groups. However, workers aged 60 and above also fared badly.

The working population

There are frontline workers who have been in the workplace throughout the pandemic and have been exposed to the greatest risks. There are many people working from home, some delighted with the flexibility this brings but others for whom this has had a detrimental effect on their mental and physical health. There are others who have been furloughing, with all the hazards this has been shown to bring.

FIGURE 16.4 Jobs changed after coronavirus outbreak, by age group: UK, April 2020

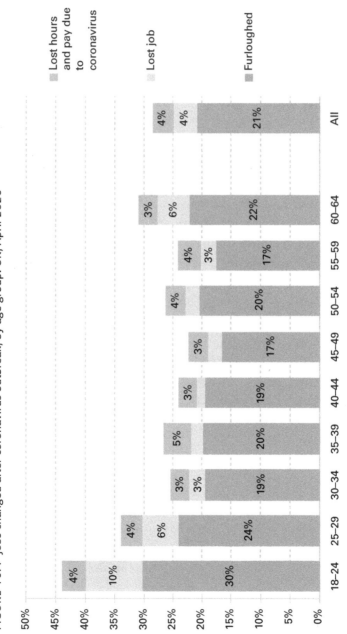

SOURCE RF analysis of ISER, Understanding Society

The distribution of already-existing chronic conditions and ill-health will fall heavily on the older worker, as will the obesity profile.

Furloughing

One in four older workers – 2.5 million in total – have been furloughed, and many of these workers may be unable to return to their previous jobs as some sectors struggle to recover: an estimated 400,000 jobs are at risk of disappearing.

Though the aims of furlough, and similar schemes to keep employees close to employment, are laudable, they may come with unintended consequences. Two reviews for the UK government, *Working for a Healthier Tomorrow* (Black, 2008) and *Psychological Wellbeing and Work* (Van Stolk et al, 2014) offer some important insights that governments and employers may wish to consider as they review the current schemes.

First, the furlough scheme currently does not allow an employee to work at all if they are part of the scheme. We know that an employee who is away from employment for a period of about six weeks becomes deconditioned. In effect, after this period it becomes much less likely that this person will return to employment. At that point, an individual is more likely to enter the benefit system.

Second, individuals who are not working may lose touch with the workplace altogether. They may be less likely to access the occupational health provision or health and wellbeing programmes offered in many workplaces. As such, people could become cut off from some of the normal support networks that may have been available to them. Without these networks, relationships at work could break down, and with them, a fundamental part of an individual's social fabric.

Third, we know that mental health tends to deteriorate when people feel that they have no social purpose. This sentiment may become more prevalent among people who are on furlough schemes where they may feel that they are kept out of work artificially or face delayed unemployment. We know that the uncertainty associated with the crisis, coupled with the disruption of routines both at home and at work, may lead to the worsening of workers' mental health. This matters. There is a strong interplay between mental health and employment. Evidence tells us that those with common mental health conditions such as anxiety and depression are much more likely to be out of employment or find it difficult to maintain employment. They are the most common conditions among those claiming out-of-work benefits, with 50 per cent of claimants typically reporting it as a primary or secondary health condition.

The pandemic has affected sectors differently: retail, hospitality, manufacturing and construction have been badly hit, as measured by the numbers furloughed. As ever it is the poorer worker who suffers most, and the older worker more than the young. The IES analysis of national data (Figure 16.5) shows very clearly the distribution across sectors (slide courtesy of Tony Wilson, Director).

Survey results

During the pandemic much material both national and from individual organizations has become available, and the voice of the older worker needs to be heard.

FIGURE 16.5   Furloughing by sector

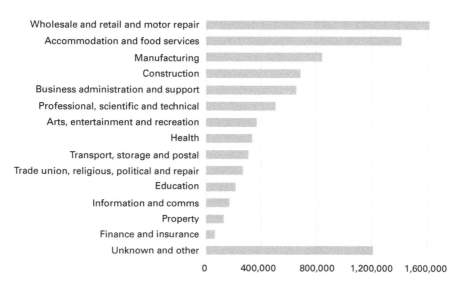

FIGURE 16.6   Financial circumstances

	Don't know	Get worse	Stay the same	Improve	Net improve
Working full time	5%	40%	49%	7%	−33
Retired	3	39%	57%	1	−37
Workless	6%	46%	42%	6%	−39
Working part time	4%	45%	48%	3	−41
Furloughed	4%	48%	46%	2	−46
Self employed	3	66%	29%	1	−65

In a recent survey by Ipsos Mori for the Centre for Ageing Better (2020) on the experience of lockdown by people approaching retirement, financial and work-related worries are evident (Figure 16.6).

Over half of people in their 50s and 60s think their finances will worsen in the year ahead, and most of those currently out of work don't expect that they'll get back into work in the future.

The self-employed figure is particularly alarming. Many older workers move to self-employment at the back end of their careers, as a way of keeping engaged and maintaining independence. We may well see a raft of healthy, productive people descending into a purposeless life, dependent on state benefits.

Around seven in ten of those who are currently workless do not feel confident that they will be employed in the future, and 44 per cent think that their finances will get worse as a result of the pandemic, rising to two-thirds of those who are self-employed.

In the same survey, views about employers varied – one in ten think that their employer has treated them differently in a negative way because of their age.

Nearly half of those in work would consider changing their working pattern as a result of the pandemic, and a quarter would consider a career change.

More data relevant to the older worker was published by the Financial Conduct Authority on 28 July 2020 (Belgibayeva et al, 2020).

FIGURE 16.7 Opinions about employers

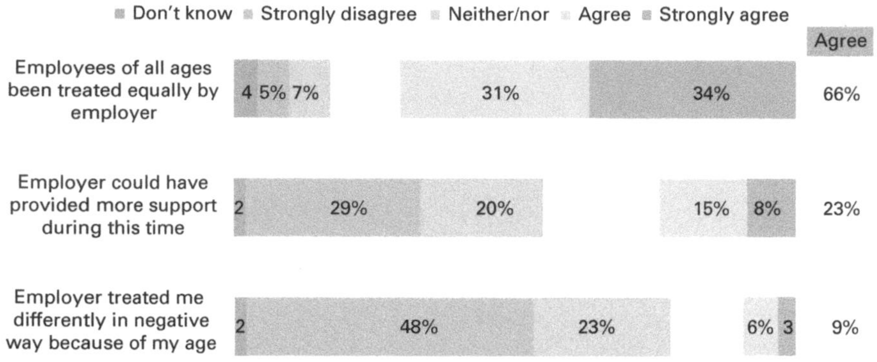

Britain's oldest workers have seen their pay fall by an average of 23 per cent, while millennials and middle-aged workers have been hit by salary cuts of 19 per cent and 17 per cent respectively. Five per cent of over-55s are working fewer hours or are on reduced pay, compared with 3 per cent of millennial and middle-aged workers. Women in their 60s, and in particular the 3.8 million impacted by the rise in the State Pension age, are experiencing greater retirement risk due to increased job losses (Thurley and McInnes, 2020).

Older workers who are yet to retire are 'now confronting real financial hardship and challenges ahead', and older people who are made redundant may get fewer opportunities to retrain (Evans, 2020). Despite 'reports that millennials have faced the worst job losses', people born between 1946 and 1964 are just as likely as 20–39-year-olds to have been made redundant during the pandemic. Six per cent of both groups have lost their jobs – three times the percentage of employees aged between 40 and 54 made redundant.

Research by the Institute for Employment Studies (Williams et al, 2020) reveals that very few employers are doing anything in their recruitment process to attract and support older workers. This can lead to older workers being less likely to re-enter the workforce. Employers should consider any ageist language used in job ads and how their general brand excludes or includes older workers, the inclusivity of the platforms on which they advertise, and application methods. CVs leave more room for bias decisions due to age cues, so application forms can be better, and using online interviews in recruitment could be a big benefit for older workers with health conditions and/or anxiety about travelling.

There is also a stereotypical view that older workers are less technologically advanced. This may fuel an idea that they are less productive when working remotely, and raises the question of whether employers should provide support to staff to adapt to new technology in an inclusive way. In 2018, 61 per cent of people without basic digital skills were female, and low-paid, part-time and older women were least likely to have essential digital skills (Lloyds Banking Group, 2019). Older female workers especially need to focus on digital skills, which two-thirds of jobs require (Sadro et al, 2021).

Prior to Covid, adjustments and support were provided to older workers with long-term health conditions, but this has not translated to the new ways of working (Williams et al, 2020). Employers are neglecting to re-evaluate or adjust their support, which could lead to people falling out of work; employers should remember and act upon their responsibility to continue to provide reasonable adjustments.

Discrimination may also raise its ugly head. The unique nature of this crisis means that there are clear risks that older people will find themselves discriminated against – inadvertently or deliberately – because employers view the greater health risk as a risk to their business, so that older people find themselves less likely to be brought back to work, more likely to be laid off, less likely to be recruited, and so on. The last time we saw employment fall for older people, in the 1980s, it was driven by deliberate early retirement policies, particularly in the then-nationalized industries.

We should also consider multiple 'lost generations'. We rightly hear a lot about the risks to those just entering the job market, and the poor prospects they face. The same is true for workers over 60 – evidence suggests that we are throwing away a vast resource of skills, experience and proven work ethic, just at a time (post-pandemic/post-Brexit) when we will need everyone to contribute if we are to build a successful, productive society. There are also softer benefits of an age-diverse workforce – the transfer of skills (especially those interpersonal skills that are being lost in a digital age), the resilience that comes from recovery from previous setbacks, and the societal cohesion created by different generations working as a team.

Disadvantaged groups

Covid has revealed a very unequal society. The pandemic is having a differential impact on a society already unequal, and those older workers who live below or near the poverty line, already deprived and with little financial security, are being thrown onto the scrap heap.

We know that the overall employment pattern for disabled people of any age has tended to mirror the overall ups and downs of the labour market. But this recession is unlike any of our recent comparators – it is driven by a virus – and a number of factors could further disadvantage people with long-term health conditions, most notably their potential vulnerability, perceived and actual, to contracting and suffering heavily from Covid-19.

Older workers may well have been in the group of individuals told by the Government to 'shield' themselves during the crisis; they will be people with chronic conditions and other risk factors. The government has asked employers to have robust measures in place for former shielders to return to work when able to do so.

Approaches and controls

Returning and supporting the older worker can be viewed both at the level of public policy and at the organizational level. In the workplace, in most settings including clinical settings, this is guided by the controls each organization employs, and also by UK and devolved-nation government and BEIS industry/sector guidance. The principles are:

- Employers should take a 'whole person approach' – balancing personal risk with the ability to introduce reasonable controls to limit exposure to Covid-19 through social distancing and amendments to work duties (such as start/finish times, periods of time spent in uncontrolled crowded areas, restricting or reducing exposure to customers and colleagues through physical distancing and workplace controls, e.g. screens or non-customer-facing zone work).

• Employer understanding and flexibility. The older worker faces a high risk of physical and mental deconditioning after as little as six weeks out of their usual work. It should be noted that these individuals are not 'unfit' for work at the current time, but a lack of physical conditioning, social interaction and sense of purpose will significantly impact on older workers' ability to return to and sustain their previous roles.

• Keep in touch. For those employees who are unable to return to work in the near future, it is recommended that a structured keep-in-touch programme (such as the process in place for new mothers) is developed, with a focus not only on the mental health risks of being away from work, but on the social connectedness and potential physical and mental deconditioning, with signposting to appropriate NHS and third-sector services.

Case studies are a great way to show what 'good' looks like, and a few examples follow, with grateful thanks to their authors, Paul Litchfield, Richard Caddis and Tony Vickers-Byrne.

CASE STUDY
BT plc

At BT, the health, safety, wellbeing and welfare of all our colleagues, whatever their age, has been the priority. Many of the operational Openreach and contact centre colleagues, being designated key workers, have remained at work, on site and in the workplace to serve customers and keep the country connected. This has included the technology solutions for the NHS and Nightingale hospitals to ensure patients are connected to their loved ones during the strict Covid restrictions.

BT's integrated health, safety and wellbeing approach has led to the development of safe systems of work, which apply the controls in place to reduce and prevent Covid transmission. It considers the individual, who is assessed against a vulnerable worker risk assessment, and a review of existing controls that are in place. Strict adherence to these controls is sufficient to reduce the risk and protect the colleague and customer where work in homes and commercial properties is completed. At the start of the pandemic, the risk was controlled further through elimination of working inside customer premises, while maintaining the ability to connect customers to broadband and telephone services. The views of individual colleagues on remaining at work, and managing the risk and controls, have been a key factor to ensure that there has been no enforced removal from work in any capacity against an employee's wishes.

From the start of the pandemic, the health, safety and wellbeing centre of expertise has run weekly webinars on a range of mental and physical health topics. Specific areas of anxiety, underlying respiratory conditions and Covid, and loneliness were discussed with the older workers' needs in mind. A functional physical conditioning, stretching and mobility toolkit – using guided online videos from registered training and musculoskeletal professionals – was introduced in June to address many months of sedentary activities and resultant deconditioning.

For those required by the government to 'shield', BT has developed a condition management programme in partnership with our mental health and physiotherapy providers. With a particular focus on safety-critical field engineers, employees who have shielded for up to four months are assessed and any mental or physical flags are managed through guided journeys of (virtual) group sessions and 1-2-1 physical reconditioning.

This has led to our colleagues and customers being kept safe as the risk from Covid changes, and has allowed our workers to remain in work with adjustments, or helped support them back to work from their period of government shielding.

CASE STUDY
Thames Water

Thames Water is the largest Water and Wastewater services provider in the United Kingdom, supplying over 15 million people. We have an active health and wellbeing strategy that is founded upon cultural norms built over the years that ensure we place the safety, health and wellbeing of our people at the heart of our business decision making.

In February, prior to the virus spreading to become a pandemic, we established a GOLD Command structure using our existing flu-pandemic plan.

This provided us with a great starting point to begin preparing our resilience measures for what was to come.

There is clear evidence indicating that vulnerability to Covid-19 increases significantly with age; for example, in comparison with a healthy person aged 20, a healthy person aged 60 has more than 30 times the risk of dying if they contract Covid-19. The protection of our older and most vulnerable workers has been a key priority for us at Thames Water since the onset of the pandemic.

To ensure we had a robust approach towards those most vulnerable, which includes older workers, we created a health assessment process at the very start of the pandemic in order to identify those who were clinically high risk due to an underlying health issue or known risk factor, all of whom were advised to refrain from work. Those who could work from home have done so throughout; for those based in the field, and unable to work from home, we chose not to use the furlough scheme and supported them through regular communications from the business.

Our comprehensive three-step assessment process takes the complexities of the medical guidance and simplifies it into a workable approach for our employees and managers. This process was firstly an employee Covid self-assessment, which went to our internal clinical team who then undertook an occupational health assessment, which was then passed to the line manager for a Covid activity-based risk assessment.

Four per cent of our workforce were originally categorized as clinically vulnerable (high risk) or clinically extremely vulnerable (very high risk/shielding) and all employees have completed the health vulnerability questionnaire and undergone the clinical assessment categorization, enabling managers to undertake the required risk assessment. Of this 4 per cent, a significant number fell into the older worker category of above 60 years of age. The approach taken ensures governance and traceability of control from an organizational perspective, and has also satisfied our insurers we have control.

CASE STUDY
Microsoft

The journey through which Covid-19 has taken many companies over the past few months has caused Microsoft to shift focus from managing health and safety in the workplace to supporting health and safety at home. With an established wellbeing programme providing physical, mental and financial wellbeing for employees with a rich suite of benefits and services to support them and their families, the priority very quickly adapted to both promoting what we already had as well as mobilizing these resources for virtual use.

As a global corporation, Microsoft was quick to react to the changing landscape as countries domino-ed into lockdown, keeping employees updated with regular, relevant and focused communications. The initial messages echoed the local UK sentiment to prioritize the health and wellbeing of employees and their loved ones.

On demographics and communities in need, we applied our growth mindset, learning from our employees through our usual communication channels, our employee resource groups, our crisis management teams and sub-teams, putting both reactive and proactive measures in place, acting with empathy and pragmatism. For the older workforce – which could include those in the vulnerable health category, with low immunity, those shielding due to the health of their partner, as well as those with children and/or older dependents – we allowed them to work from home or reviewed options for those whose attendance on site was necessary according to their role (essential workers at our data centres or retail store employees).

Other communities in need soon became apparent – as schools and childcare facilities closed, Microsoft moved at speed to grant 12 weeks of paid pandemic school and childcare closure leave in addition to the caregiver leave our policies already supported.

In contrast to the challenge of managing care for children or elderly relatives, we learnt from those living alone of their own challenges – of loneliness, of work and home blending into one, of a disinclination to take time off from work as during the initial lockdown. They faced days or weeks alone without even the social aspect of work to distract them.

We produced a Working from Home Wellbeing Guide – with Top Tips on managing physical and mental wellbeing during lockdown. Our wellbeing team worked with our benefits providers to deliver live and recorded webinars, to educate and inform employees on how best to manage stress and anxiety, coping with bereavement and loss, and looking after their workstation and posture. Our employees contributed with their own stories of how they were managing work and home life during lockdown, sharing their own ideas and tips.

To support those who might have been impacted financially during the pandemic, we followed up with a Financial Wellbeing guide, providing FAQs on how those nearing retirement might be impacted with regard to pensions and savings, and again, practical guidance on how to manage pension contributions, and other ways to review and manage budgets and savings at this time.

Microsoft as a technology company is, in some ways, blessed, in that we already had a fairly flexible working culture, our own products and applications to support a full-time working from home model, and a diverse workforce with a wide demographic of ages. We continue to support by listening to and learning from our employees, and ensuring they have access to our resources when they need them.

Public policy and practice

This short paper and analysis raises questions about public policy and practice, for example in the design of future furlough/short-time-working support; in implementing better support programmes for those out of work; promoting workplace health support, Access to Work, better protections for insecure workers, better enforcement of employment protections etc. These are questions for government but also for us to think about when considering specific measures in response to the crisis.

References

Belgibayeva, A et al (2020) Coronavirus and intergenerational difference – the emerging picture, FCA, https://www.fca.org.uk/insight/coronavirus-and-intergenerational-difference-emerging-picture (archived at https://perma.cc/6SFL-ZBQA)

Black, C (2008) Working for a Healthier Tomorrow, GOV.UK, www.gov.uk/government/publications/working-for-a-healthier-tomorrow-work-and-health-in-britain (archived at https://perma.cc/AA5B-G6Y4)

Centre for Ageing Better (2020) State of Ageing in 2020, https://www.ageing-better.org.uk/summary-state-ageing-2020 (archived at https://perma.cc/52NA-ZBSB)

Dixon, A et al (2020) The experience of people approaching later life in lockdown, Centre for Ageing Better, https://www.ageing-better.org.uk/events/ipsos-mori-impact-covid-19-webinar (archived at https://perma.cc/FJ83-BPHW)

Evans, J (2020) Coronavirus: Over-55s main victims of employment crisis, watchdog finds, *The Week*, https://www.theweek.co.uk/107643/over-55s-main-victims-of-coronavirus-job-crisis (archived at https://perma.cc/WN67-KNJW)

Lloyds Bank (2019) Lloyds Bank UK Consumer Digital Index 2019, https://www.digital-champion.co.uk/lloyds-bank-uk-consumer-digital-index-2019/ (archived at https://perma.cc/Y4ET-G9GF)

NatCen Social Research, https://www.natcen.ac.uk/ (archived at https://perma.cc/B2HQ-DVS4)

Official Labour Force Survey, https://www.ons.gov.uk/surveys/informationforhouseholdsandindividuals/householdandindividualsurveys/labourforcesurvey (archived at https://perma.cc/CUC4-BJS9)

Office for National Statistics (nd), https://www.ons.gov.uk/ (archived at https://perma.cc/22QP-QGF5)

Resolution Foundation (2020) The Full Monty: Facing up to the scale of the COVID-19 jobs crisis, https://www.resolutionfoundation.org/events/the-full-monty/ (archived at https://perma.cc/QW5G-Q7MY)

Sadro, F et al (2021) What works for adult online learning: An evaluation of the CareerTech Challenge, Nesta, https://www.nesta.org.uk/report/what-works-adult-online-learning-evaluation-careertech-challenge/ (archived at https://perma.cc/Z4YU-W48X)

Thurley, D and McInnes, R (2020) State Pension age increases for women born in the 1950s, Paper No CBP-7405, https://researchbriefings.files.parliament.uk/documents/CBP-7405/CBP-7405.pdf (archived at https://perma.cc/FC7R-CTZF)

Understanding Society (nd), https://www.understandingsociety.ac.uk/ (archived at https://perma.cc/2N9F-44TK)

van Stolk, C et al (2014) Psychological Wellbeing and Work, https://www.base-uk.org/sites/default/files/knowledge/Psychological%20Wellbeing%20and%20Work:%20Improving%20Service%20Provision%20and%20Outcomes%20for%20People%20With%20Mental%20Health%20Problems%20in%20the%20UK/psychological-wellbeing-and-work.pdf (archived at https://perma.cc/U8B6-BN9N)

Williams, M et al (2020) The impacts of the coronavirus crisis on the labour market: Analysis of quarterly Labour Force Survey data, Institute for Employment Studies, https://www.employment-studies.co.uk/resource/impacts-coronavirus-crisis-labour-market (archived at https://perma.cc/63TQ-8DNB)

17

Concluding remarks

We have previously written about designing, implementing and evaluating effective wellbeing strategy (Hesketh and Cooper, 2019). Clearly organizations that have followed our previous submissions have been prepared to address the tsunami of issues that have arisen out of the pandemic. Some of that good practice is clear to see in the narratives of our Forum members described here. While it is clear the pandemic has had a catastrophic impact on every walk of life, it is also clear that it has been a period of unprecedented development, at pace. Technology has expanded into almost every home in the land; it is accepted that business can be done, if not ideally, online. Communications do not always need to be in person and unnecessary business travel has been reduced by its largest margin ever. It has been described as the largest social experiment, albeit forced, ever conducted. Our way of life has changed beyond recognition, but will that remain the case as the country enters a period of recovery?

During the first year of the pandemic Forum members began to ask each other in the search for solutions (the key aim of the Forum being to share good or promising practice), how are others approaching the return to office for workers who have been working all this time from home? For example, will people be expected to go back at all? What prioritization is in place? What psychological support is being offered for those continuing in the workplace and those set to return to it?

A further line of inquiry asked, do members have any advice on how to communicate to our managers and employees around the importance of taking time out from work and using their annual leave to rest and recuperate (despite holiday bookings being cancelled)? In the CIPD Wellbeing Survey (CIPD, 2021) the overwhelming majority of respondents (84 per cent) have observed 'presenteeism', both in the workplace (75 per cent) and while working at home (77 per cent), over the past 12 months. Further, seven in ten (70 per cent) have observed some form of 'leaveism', such as working outside contracted hours or using holiday entitlement to work, over the past 12 months. While it was reported that more organizations are taking steps to address both 'presenteeism' and 'leaveism' compared with last year, over two-fifths of those experiencing these issues are not taking any action (43 per cent for those experiencing presenteeism; 47 per cent in the case of leaveism). In the hybrid model described next, this will have to be addressed by managers.

As previously mentioned, we suspect some sort of hybrid working model will eventually emerge, somewhere between pre-pandemic and peri-pandemic practices. Within this we will consider some of the key challenges that have stood out in our previous chapters.

Working from home – the challenges

In terms of working from home, it is evident that Covid-19 may well have forced a new working paradigm. How long this will persist is yet unknown. Some of the challenges have been laid out in the previous chapters. From the very start, the immediate challenge for most organizations was to move quickly to home-working solutions or take decisions to furlough huge chunks of their most precious resource: their people. It was immediately clear, as attested in many of these accounts, that a pressing need was to assist managers with managing their now remote teams; employees needed advice, guidance and equipment to enable remote working.

The challenges of working from home are numerous. Consideration needs to be given to wellbeing and productivity, especially the expectations and behaviours of managers. One consideration would be that people who previously may have wanted to work flexibly and/or remotely had been less inclined to ask due to fears around job security or how it may adversely affect their career, promotion or development opportunities. The Covid working-from-home direction has provided an opportunity for employees to illustrate they can be as productive, if not more so, while working from home. They are afforded more time to be at home, the flexibility of being able to work when convenient, and have more disposable hours due to savings on commute times. In the piece from JLL, they conceded that they had moved into people's private spheres, their homes. However, they found that people discovered emotions and started to speak more, sharing when they were feeling good or awful. People spoke more about their wellbeing and were more accepting of others. We may contrast this with a consideration that younger people, who may not have their own homes and may have to share small spaces, equipment and Wi-Fi with others, may not be able to work effectively from home. These younger workers may well benefit from a return to a place to work from that is not their home.

Furloughing

There is a potential financial lurking as furlough payments have now ceased. It is unclear at this stage what may come, but a recession seems likely and wellbeing is becoming a critical strategic priority. Small to medium enterprises have been supported well during the pandemic, but with many moving parts and a shifting workforce, many anticipate significant disruption to the economy. This may be compounded by employees feeling job insecure, and as previously mentioned, the criticality of good management cannot be stressed enough. The issues surrounding Brexit and how that will impact on trade more generally post-pandemic are also an area of huge concern for organizations.

Shielding, isolating and the challenge of track and trace

All of these issues have provided major challenges to all organizations as they have battled against the pandemic. The endless amendments to the advice, guidance or mandates, dependent on where you are in the country, have been the cause of many a management headache. As the world enters the recovery phase, wrestling these measures has not become easier. The matter of compliance is not getting any clearer and we have seen example upon example of high-profile people being caught out by the rules at the existing time. Some have been blatant breaches, but many quite unintentional. As those responsible for organizational compliance at any point in time, it has been the source of much anxiety and stress. The majority of organizations contributing to this book have premises spread around the globe, let alone in different towns where the rules may be quite different. For managers, it is clear that there needs to be clarity for the workforce and full support when their employees have to shield, isolate, or (yet another new term) have been 'pinged' by track and trace.

Being a good manager – key takeaways

Good management is critical to successful employee wellbeing. A key part to this is good engagement on a regular basis. We have heard numerous examples in these accounts of great organizational engagement. Managers need to know how employees are feeling about their work; they need to make regular contact, particularly with those they do not see in the course of the working day. The pandemic has shone a light on home working efficacy, and there appear to be mixed views. Some organizations are intent on a full 'back to normal' picture, while others are keen to embrace a new more flexible way of working. The second way requires both employers and employees to have trust and autonomy. Managers need to tune into how to remotely manage effectively, balancing feelings of isolation with feelings of being micromanaged. Managers are required to adopt new styles, agree 'the deal' with their employees and then keep these 'contracts' authentically. Regular staff surveys are an ideal way to complement regular management contact; however, managers need to take note of what employees are telling them, and all too often this is simply not the case. The survey itself is not the objective. Any subsequent interventions must be carefully considered and put in place. Small-scale pilots are a good way to test thinking, but again they need to be thoughtfully evaluated before making them business as usual. Managers need to have the ability to acknowledge when things are not working, as well as when they are. Managers, or leaders, need to have the ability to cope with the current uncertainty, as in the VUCA model by George Casey mentioned by Andy Rhodes in Chapter 3. Warren Bennis is attributed to have said leadership is like beauty – it is hard to define but you know it when you see it. We would suggest that in terms of remote/home working this extends to how workers feel about their working life, and we know that managers have the biggest impact on this. We have often said that people join organizations but leave managers.

What also comes through loud and clear from the accounts is that use of remote working solutions has spiralled. Managers need to be really careful in their expectations of a remote workforce and/or of people working flexibly. As we have discussed, emails are a big tell here; managers should not routinely expect employees to be viewing, responding to or sending emails outside of working hours. CIPD have reported increased instances of both presenteeism and leaveism behaviours during the pandemic and it is clear this must be reduced. Are people sending, receiving or responding to emails when not at work because they are worried about their jobs? Are they sending emails because their managers don't know if they are working or not, as some sort of proof they are? When working from home, employees must be given adequate breaks and periods of rest. Ensure also that days off and annual leave are honoured and taken.

To conclude, dealing with wellbeing strategically is now even more important than ever, given the continuing health crisis, which is not going to go away. On top of this is a looming recession and then there's the yet unknown impact of Brexit or even the survival of the

EU. More than ever before we are going to need socially intelligent line managers. They need to be equipped to manage people who are working in a hybrid model. They need to be able to spot signs of ill health, but often online. So, they need to be looking out for strange behaviours, signs of presenteeism and leaveism, signs of job insecurity, not taking time off or working strange hours for no apparent reason, not using their holidays and so on. They also need to be able to intervene quickly and effectively if they hear or see any of these behaviours playing out. Great managers speak to their direct reports at least once a week. This doesn't even have to be about work, it is just a chance to have a chat and ensure everything is okay, enquiring if they are taking regular breaks, having lunch and getting some exercise. It is also okay not to be okay. Great managers expect to hear this and are equipped to respond in a positive and compassionate way. The pandemic has thrown up many curve balls and never has there been such a critical time to champion great managers, have a positive and inclusive working environment, and promote and strive for a resilient workforce.

Finally, we hope the accounts in this book have inspired you with new ideas to test or use in your own workplace, wherever that may be. The last years have been an enormous challenge for all organizations. We hope the many views illustrated here will show just how much of a challenge it has been across all occupations for many different reasons. There is a huge opportunity to emerge from the pandemic with better working practices that support employees to draw meaning and purpose from their life and to experience lots of good days at work.

References

CIPD (2021) Health and Wellbeing at Work Survey 2021, Chartered Institute of Personnel and Development, London, https://www.cipd.co.uk/Images/health-wellbeing-work-report-2021_tcm18-93541.pdf (archived at https://perma.cc/7XT2-WCMJ)

Hesketh, I and Cooper, C (2019) Wellbeing at Work: How to design, implement and evaluate an effective strategy, Kogan Page, London

INDEX

CPSIA information can be obtained
at www.ICGtesting.com
Printed in the USA
BVHW021754271221
624947BV00003B/50